Creative Gre

Life
Preservers

God's Promises for Troubled Times

13
Complete
Lessons

Adapted for Group Study by Jan Johnson

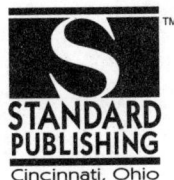

STANDARD
PUBLISHING
Cincinnati, Ohio

Creative Groups Guide: Life Preservers

By Jan Johnson

Edited by Michael C. Mack, The Small Group Network, Inc. (http://smallgroups.com).

Cover design by SchultzWard, Inc.

The Standard Publishing Company, Cincinnati, Ohio.
A division of Standex International Corporation.

04 03 02 01 00 99 98 97   5 4 3 2 1

ISBN 0-7847-0574-7

ontents

Foreword

"I promise."

In a hedonistic world where people would rather do what they feel like doing than keep their word, that phrase may seem pretty meaningless—unless the promise comes from a loving father.

We have a perfect heavenly Father. Is there anyone on earth as loving and unselfish as God? Does anyone care more about you than he does? Is there anyone who is more true to his word? Is there anyone who has sacrificed more for you? When God makes a promise, you can believe he will do what he says—no matter what. And God has made many promises to you.

God especially wants you to be comforted during difficult times. He knows that this world is full of heartaches. He knows you will need special assurance from him in times of need.

This book examines those promises, which were first revealed in his love letter to you called the Bible. You may occasionally be surprised by what God promises you. But it is always refreshing to know the truth, and to know exactly what God is going to do for you in your time of need.

"The one who calls you is faithful and he will do it" (1 Thessalonians 5:24).

"God, who has called you into fellowship with his Son Jesus Christ our Lord, is faithful" (1 Corinthians 1:9).

"The Lord is not slow in keeping his promise" (2 Peter 3:9).

"If we are faithless, he will remain faithful, for he cannot disown himself" (2 Timothy 2:13).

—Bob Russell

Introduction

Welcome to Creative Groups Guides!

Whether your group meets in a classroom at the church building or in the family room in someone's home, this guide will help you get the most out of your session.

You can use this Creative Groups Guide with or without *Life Preservers*, the companion book written by Bob Russell. Use this guide even if you haven't read that book. But if you do read it, you'll be even more equipped for leading the group.

Each section in this guide includes two plans—one for classes and one for small groups. This gives the leader several options:

• Use the plan just as it is written. If you teach an adult Sunday school or an elective class, use Plan One. If you lead a small group, use Plan Two.

• Perhaps you teach a Sunday school class that prefers a small group style of teaching. Use the discussion questions and activities in Plan Two, but don't overlook the great ideas presented in Plan One. Mix and match the two plans to suit your class.

• Use the best of both plans. Perhaps you could start off your class with a discussion activity in Plan Two, and then use the Bible-study section in Plan One. Use the accountability, worship, or memory verse options presented in Plan Two in your Sunday school class. Use some of the "Sunday school" activities and resource sheets presented in Plan One in your small group meeting. Variety is the spice of life!

Resource sheets in each session are available for you to tear out and photocopy for your class or group. Overhead transparency masters are also included for most sessions. Use your own creativity as you decide how to make these resources work for you.

This guide has been developed to help you do several things. First, you'll be able to facilitate active and interactive learning. These methods help students remember and put into practice what they learn. Second, you'll help your class or group apply the lessons to their lives. These sessions will help your group members actually do something with what they're studying. Third, we've given you lots of options. Only you know what will work best in your class or group. Finally, support and encouragement are integrated into each session. Learning and application happen best when participants are helping one another. That may mean accountability if your group has built up the trust and caring it takes, or it may simply mean that people are lovingly encouraging one another to continue growing in knowledge and action.

How to Use This Guide

Each session begins with an excerpt from *Life Preservers*. This excerpt summarizes the session at a glance. Use it in your preparation or read it to your class or group as an introduction to a session. The central theme and lesson aims help you understand the main ideas being presented and what outcomes you are looking for.

Materials you might need on hand to conduct your session are listed on the first page of each of the plans.

In both plans, there are three main parts to each session: Building Community, a warm-up activity or icebreaker question; Considering Scripture, Bible-study activities and discussion; and Taking the Next Step, activities or discussion that will help participants apply what they have learned.

In Plan One for classes, the names of activities are listed in the margins, along with the suggested time for each one. Use these as you plan your lesson and as you teach to stay on track. In most cases, optional activities are listed. Use these instead of or in addition to other activities as time allows.

A number of options are included in Plan Two for groups. Use the accountability-partner option to help the group support, encourage, and hold one another accountable. This works particularly well in a group in which trust has already been gained between participants. Accountability partners can help one another put what they are learning each week into practice. They can pray with and for each other throughout the week. They can "spur one another on toward love and good deeds" (Hebrews 10:24).

Other options include worship ideas and a memory verse. Use these at your discretion to help your group grow in love, devotion, and praise for God and for hiding his Word in their hearts.

Use this guide to help you prepare, but we suggest that you do not take this book to your class or group meeting and merely read from it. Instead, take notes on a separate sheet of paper and use that as you lead your group.

One

God's Promises in Times of Fear

*I*t is said that we are born with only two fears: the fear of falling and the fear of loud noises. All other fears are learned or acquired. When we reach adulthood, our fears become more sophisticated. Instead of the bogeyman, we fear the IRS man or the policeman. Instead of strange noises in the closet, we have skeletons in the closet. We may not believe in ghosts, but we do fear death. And we still fear being left alone.

Has God called you to do something specific that is frightening? Start a family? Break a sinful habit? Confront a family member? Heal a broken relationship? Take a new job? Start a business? Enter the ministry?

Someone said that courage is not the absence of fear, but action in spite of fear. Seek the reassurance of other believers. Have faith in God's promise and not your own power.

—Adapted from *Life Preservers*, by Bob Russell

Central Theme	God provides the means by which we can overcome fear.
Lesson Aim	Group members will examine the biblical means God provides for overcoming fears and explore past fearful situations to discover how God helped them.
Bible Background	Joshua 1:1–9; 2:1, 8–11; 3:5, 6, 13–17
For Further Study	Read Chapter 1 of *Life Preservers*.

Classes

BUILDING COMMUNITY

Have class members divide into groups of four members or fewer and say, **Tell the group two things you've done or said that seemed too difficult at the time. One of the things, however, should be false—you didn't really do it, but try to sound convincing. After the first one in your group shares, the rest of your group can try to guess which one was a lie. Continue that way with the other group members.**

Have class members form small groups and tell each other something they've done that they were afraid to do at the time. If there's still time after everyone has had a turn, have each member take another turn to answer this question: **How did God provide me the courage to do the thing I mentioned?**

Summarize this way after either activity: **Today's session focuses on Joshua, who was given a difficult command. He could have easily decided it required too much courage or that he was too afraid to obey, but God provided him several means of help.**

CONSIDERING SCRIPTURE

Before class, ask a skilled reader to skim the following passages to read them aloud at this point in class: *Joshua 1:1–9; 2:1, 8–13; and 3:8, 13–17.* Before you call on this volunteer to read, divide the class into two teams, designating one as "pessimists" and the other as "optimists." Distribute copies of Resource Sheet 1A, "Slanted Listening," and explain that as the volunteer reads aloud, the teams should listen for cues to their group theme. Read aloud what is on Resource Sheet 1A below the titles "pessimists" and "optimists" to make sure class members understand what is wanted. After the Scripture has been read, ask the "pessimists" and "optimists" to share their ideas.

As the "pessimists" and "optimists" share their ideas, provide this enrichment.
Pessimists: Pass out copies of Resource Sheet 1B, "Reasons Joshua Could Have Been Afraid." Ask a volunteer to read it

One Fact, One Lie
10 Minutes

OPTION
Group Sharing
5–10 Minutes

Materials You'll Need For This Session

Resource Sheets 1A and 1B, Transparency 1A, pens or pencils, colored pen for transparency, chalk and chalkboard

Listening Teams
10 Minutes

OPTION
Further Clarification of Ideas
10 Minutes

aloud, noting afterward that we often minimize the real fears that biblical figures must have had. They didn't know they were heroes!

Optimists: Ask them to share their ideas while you display Transparency 1A, "Taming Those Fears." As they offer ideas, fill in their answers on the transparency under the appropriate categories (listed below) behind the words: Example from Scripture.

If they miss any of these ideas, include these and the explanations that follow.

The testimony of others: Rahab

Explain if necessary that her fear showed the Israelites how powerful and dangerous they appeared to others.

The support of godly leaders: the priests

The priests respected Joshua enough to stand in the flood stage river water with the Ark of the Covenant. They didn't complain about how it might look sacrilegious (3:15–17).

Unexplainable circumstances: the miraculous crossing of the Jordan on dry ground

This miraculous crossing showed God's power and reminded the Israelites of their mission, because, like them, their relatives had crossed the Red Sea and found freedom from slavery (3:15–17).

Summarize by saying, **God doesn't give commands that are too difficult, even though they look that way. God supplies what is needed.**

OPTION
Sing-down
15 Minutes

If you have action-oriented class members, consider using the listening teams, but instead of having them simply tell their answers, do the following. The "pessimists" begin by presenting their first reason to the tune of a well-known folk song or childhood song. (Choose this before class. For example, they could use the tune of the folk song, "Michael, Row the Boat Ashore," but replace "Alleluia," with something like, "Joshua should have been afraid" or "Joshua wasn't afraid." They can sing their reason in the first and third line.)

After the "pessimists" have presented one reason, the "optimists" should immediately present one using the same song. Go back and forth until one group can think of no other reasons. If you use Resource Sheet 1B and Transparency 1A, don't do so until after the sing-down.

TAKING THE NEXT STEP

Challenge class members to consider how they can seek out these elements that God provided. Sometimes God provides them, but we're not alert enough to see them.

Leave Transparency 1A on display so you can challenge class members to consider how these steps can help them overcome their fears. Underline the three numbered questions with a colored pen.

Ask class members to pick a partner with whom they feel somewhat comfortable (although it might be better for spouses not to be partners) so they can interview each other. Explain, **Start by thinking of something you're afraid to do—take a new job, break a habit, heal a broken relationship, start a business, start a family. You don't need to say aloud what that fear is—you can even call it "X." Then one partner should ask the other Questions 1, 2, and 3 from Transparency 1A. Then change roles. When it's your turn to be the questioner, listen carefully and offer very little feedback so the answerer can have as much time as possible.**

After about five minutes, ask the partners to reverse the process with the one who answered now asking the questions.

Distribute paper and pencil (or ask class members to use the back of one of the resource sheets), and have class members answer the three numbered questions on Transparency 1A individually. If you don't want to display the transparency, you can write the questions on the chalkboard.

Close in prayer, asking God to help class members remain alert to the ways that God provides the means and power to overcome fears.

Following either of the above activities, ask volunteers to share any surprises that occurred to them regarding how God had helped them. After one or two class members share their thoughts, ask each person to consider which of the three means of support (listed on Transparency 1A) he or she needs to pay more attention to in the future.

PLAN TWO

Groups

BUILDING COMMUNITY

1. When have you done something, even though you were afraid to do it?

2. It's been said, "Courage is not the absence of fear, but action in spite of fear." What gave you courage in those circumstances (from Question 1)?

3. OPTION: Skip question 2 and say instead, **Indicate by a show of hands if you were positively influenced by:**
  • **the example of someone who had been through a similar situation**
  • **the example of someone who was a leader to you**
  • **the words of someone who was a leader to you**
  • **unusual circumstances**
  • **other (ask them to tell what)**

CONSIDERING SCRIPTURE

Read Joshua 1:1–9.

1. Whose place was Joshua taking and why could that have been intimidating for him? (Especially after his death, Moses probably became a legend. He had been instrumental in so many miracles—crossing the Red Sea, the miraculous manna and quail, the procuring of water from a rock. He had been their judge and spiritual leader.)

2. What promises did God make to Joshua? (See 1:3–5.)

3. What instructions did God give Joshua? (Among the instructions listed in 1:6–9, God told Joshua three times to be strong and courageous.)

Read Joshua 2:1, 8–13.

4. How could the request of Rahab the prostitute have served as a source of courage to the spies? (Her request for amnesty [vv. 12, 13] showed her fear and indicated that Jericho must have

OPTION
Accountability Partners
Have accountability partners meet during the week to discuss how alert they are to ways that God helps them overcome fears. It would be helpful to talk about their fears for a few minutes and then share the supports that are helping them. Encourage them that even though they may feel they have no fears or no ways of overcoming the ones they have, the talking will help them consider these things.

OPTION
Worship Ideas
Read Psalm 34 together as an act of worship.

OPTION
Memory Verse
"Have I not commanded you? Be strong and courageous. Do not be terrified; do not be discouraged, for the Lord your God will be with you wherever you go" (Joshua 1:9).

been intimidated by the Israelites. This probably gave the Israelites courage to hear that God had fought so hard for them that they scared a whole group of people.)

5. What was it about Israel that made Jericho so afraid? (The miracles showed that God was with Israel and he was a God who—unlike the false gods—was very present in Heaven and earth!)

Read Joshua 3:8 13–17.

6. What instructions were passed from God to Joshua to the priests? (For the priests to stand in the middle of the river showed that they respected Joshua and equated his odd request with the will of God.)

7. Describe the miracle that occurred.

OPTION Skim ahead in Joshua.

8. What great things did Joshua go on to do?
(Two highlights were Joshua's leading in the battle of Jericho [chapters 5 and 6] and the battle against the Amorites in which God rained hailstones on them and caused the sun to stand still [chapter 10].)

TAKING THE NEXT STEP

1. Have you been helped by any of these supports?
   • **the testimony of others**
   • **the support of godly leaders**
   • **unexplainable circumstances**
If so, tell us about it.

2. Which, if any, of those supports have you experienced lately? How?

3. What fears do you have about leading out for God? (Offer these examples of leading out: taking a new job, breaking a habit, healing a broken relationship, starting a business, starting a family.) **Which, if any, of those supports do you need to overcome that fear?**

Slanted Listening

Joshua 1:1–9; 2:1, 8–13; 3:8, 13–17

PESSIMISTS	OPTIMISTS
Listen for reasons Joshua could have been afraid or intimidated.	Listen for the means God provided to keep Joshua from being afraid. What did God do or use to do this?

Reasons Joshua Could Have Been Afraid

Joshua was following a legend.

It is difficult to follow a legend. Ask Gene Bartow who resigned from the head basketball coaching job at UCLA after two winning seasons. The pressure from the media and fans was oppressive. His record would have been acceptable any place else, but he was following the legendary John Wooden who had won ten national championships.

Joshua was following a legend. Moses had led the people of Israel for forty years. Moses had rescued them from Egypt, crossed the Red Sea, brought them the Ten Commandments. He had been their judge and their spiritual leader. He had walked and talked with God. Would the people be willing to follow Joshua as they had Moses?

Joshua had witnessed a previous failure.

Forty years earlier the Israelites had been in the same situation. Instead of being strong and courageous, they got cold feet. When they should have been focusing on the faithfulness of God's promises, they focused on the size of the people. Joshua had been there. He was one of only two (Caleb was the other) who believed in the power of God and trusted the Lord to give them victory. As a result, he and Caleb were the only ones of that generation God left alive to enter the Promised Land. Would this younger generation get cold feet as their parents did?

Sometimes experience can be a detriment. Older people know the dangers that lie ahead. That is why young people are often more bold than those who have experienced life's successes and failures. More experienced folk tend to be cynical.

Joshua had not performed miracles.

Whenever Israel came into great difficulty, Moses had displayed miraculous powers. Would God work through Joshua as well? What if they came to the Jordan River and the rod didn't work? Did Joshua have the faith in God he needed? Did God truly have confidence in Joshua as the chosen leader?

The enemy forces were intimidating.

Joshua and Caleb were the only ones who had been to the Promised Land and experienced what the land was really like. Yes, they had focused on the wonders of the land that would someday be theirs. But in the back of their minds they knew that the other ten spies were right: the cities were well fortified and the people were like giants.

The Israelites had little battle experience.

The Israelites were not battle-hardened. They would be fighting against Canaanite nations who were used to war. Joshua would have to face the mothers and wives of those who died in battle. Would the Israelite armies have to go through the "school of hard knocks" before they were victorious?

—Adapted from *Life Preservers,* by Bob Russell

Taming Those Fears

God helps us overcome fear through . . .

✦ *the testimony of others*

Example from Scripture:

1. Who has been through something similar and might be able to help you, if you approached him or her?

✦ *the support of godly leaders*

Example from Scripture:

2. What godly person (who is a leader to you) could you consult for ideas and encouragement?

✦ *unexplainable circumstances*

Example from Scripture:

3. In what ways has God already provided unexplainable circumstances, resources, or people who have helped you?

Two

God's Promises in Times of Doubt

*T*here are three ways we can approach God: belief, doubt, and unbelief. Belief and unbelief are choices. Doubt is an honest expression. You can feel doubt during a sincere search for the truth. God loves the honest searcher and will patiently reveal himself to the one who seeks him.

The Bible makes a clear distinction between the person who is an unbeliever and the person who has occasional doubts during difficult times in life. Psalm 14:1 condemns the atheist as a fool: "The fool says in his heart, 'There is no God.'" Yet, Jesus, while he often bemoaned the lack of faith of his disciples, was patient with those with doubts and continually tried to strengthen their faith. It is comforting to witness in Scripture God's promises to his servants who experienced the same struggles with doubt.

—Adapted from *Life Preservers*, by Bob Russell

Central Theme	God works with us to help us resolve our doubts.
Lesson Aim	Group members will discover biblical principles for working through doubts and choose specific ways to address their doubts.
Bible Background	Judges 6:11–23; 6:36–7:15
For Further Study	Read Chapter 2 of *Life Preservers*.

Classes

BUILDING COMMUNITY

Display <u>Transparency 2A</u>, "Doubting Styles," and underline one of the recurring thoughts at the top—the one you think would seem most farfetched to your group. Say, **Let's say you kept getting recurring thoughts that it would be a good idea to . . .** (point to the thought you underlined). Pick a class member and say his or her name. **_____ , into which of these categories would you probably fit?** (Point to the cartoon faces.) Call on several other class members, changing the recurring thought if you wish, or adding your own idea.

Ask class members to choose partners and say, **In what period of your life have you had the most doubts—that God was with you, that he was leading you into some venture, that he would get you through something? Think of that time and take about two or three minutes to tell your partner.** If you wish, elaborate by suggesting these life stages: childhood, teens, leaving home, starting to work, getting married, buying a car or home, having kids, changing jobs.

CONSIDERING SCRIPTURE

Ask class members to turn to **_Judges 6_** and distribute copies of <u>Resource Sheet 2A</u>, "Tour Map Through Gideon's Doubts." Have a volunteer read the Scene 1 passage and then ask class members to describe Gideon's doubts and God's response. Before beginning Scene 2, read the inserted material about Judges 6:24–35. Then go on to Scene 2 and continue through the sheet.

Here are some responses class members might offer.

Judges 6:11–23: _Gideon's doubts_ were evidenced by his incredulous statements to the angel (vv. 13, 15, 17). He not only "talked back" to the angel, but begged for a sign. _God responded_ (through the angel) to the "back talk" by challenging Gideon to lead the people. He responded to the request for a sign by giving it—the fire consuming meat and unleavened bread (v. 21).

Judges 6:36–40: _Gideon's doubts_ were expressed by his request for two more signs with the fleece. _God responded_ by complying.

Judges 7:1–8: _Gideon_ seems to have shown no doubts in this

Choosing Styles
5 Minutes

OPTION
Neighbor Nudge
5–10 Minutes

Scripture Search
15 Minutes

Materials You'll Need For This Session

Resource Sheets 2A–2C, Transparency 2A, pens or pencils, chalk and chalkboard passage even when God challenged him to pair down his army from 32,000 to 300. *God responded* by giving him further challenges.

Judges 7:9–15: *Gideon's doubts* show in his apparent fear to attack (v. 10). *God responded* by anticipating those fears and allowing Gideon to overhear a conversation in which a dream is interpreted to mean that Gideon will conquer the Midianites.

OPTION
Continuum Evaluation
10–15 Minutes

Draw a horizontal line across the chalkboard. On the left end, write "impatient," and on the right end, write "patient." After having a volunteer read each passage section (Judges 6:11–23; 6:36–40; 7:1–8; 7:9–15), ask this question: **How patient would you say God was with Gideon and his doubts?** Let class members come up and mark on the continuum where they would put God's patience as evidenced in that passage. Then ask them to give evidence from the text to support their ideas. After the last section, point out that although God was patient—to the point of anticipating Gideon's fears (Judges 7:10)—God challenged Gideon both with chopping down the Asherah pole and by paring down his forces.

OPTION
Summary Question
5 Minutes

Use the continuum evaluation question above as a summary for the Scripture Search without going over every passage again.

OPTION
**Measuring Cultural
Myths Against Scripture**
5–10 Minutes

Distribute photocopies of Resource Sheet 2B, "What Does God Do with Doubters?" Under point one, Bob Russell says, "We sometimes falsely imagine God as someone who is standing by ready to condemn us the first time we doubt his word." Ask class members how someone with that mind-set would imagine that God would respond to these statements by Gideon:

- **"If the Lord is with us, why has all this happened to us? . . . The Lord has abandoned us and put us into the hand of Midian"** (Judges 6:13).
- **"Do not be angry with me. Let me make just one more request"** (Judges 6:39).

After hearing class members' responses, ask, **Does this false idea that God is ready to condemn us the first time we doubt his word help us with our doubts or hinder us?** Make it clear that a true understanding of God can help us with doubts.

TAKING THE NEXT STEP

Scene Planning
15 Minutes

Ask class members to form groups of two or three, and distribute a copy of Resource Sheet 2C, "Tell Me a Story," to each group. Read the instructions together. Let them know that

This doesn't have to be as outstanding a story as Gideon's. You can deal with everyday issues and everyday Christians learning to trust God more. If they find it easier to make up a story without using the outline on the sheet or adjusting it a great deal, that's fine too.

As they work, remind them of the topics on Resource Sheet 2B, if you've already used it—that God is patient with honest doubters and that he offers evidence to sincere seekers.

Distribute photocopies of Resource Sheet 2B, "What Does God Do with Doubters?" if you haven't already. Have a volunteer read it. Ask class members to underline anything that speaks to doubts they have now or have had in the past. Give them a minute or two, and then ask them to turn the sheet over and write on the back a prayer to God, admitting their doubts and asking for God's guidance in overcoming them.

OPTION
Prayer Writing
5 Minutes

PLAN TWO

Groups

BUILDING COMMUNITY

1. When you think of doubt, what color do you think of?

2. Is doubt the same as unbelief? How are they the same or different?

3. OPTION: **If you were going to have doubts about anything concerning God, what would it be?**

CONSIDERING SCRIPTURE

Read Judges 6:11–23.

1. **What doubts did Gideon express when he responded to the angel's greeting?**

2. **What evidence does the text offer that the angel was or was not offended by Gideon's statement that the Lord had abandoned Israel?**

3. **Do you think Gideon knew who the angel was? Offer evidence from the text.** (Yes: He called the angel "Lord" [v. 15]. No: Gideon called the angel "sir" and referred to the Lord as someone else [v. 13]; he wanted a sign that the angel was really God. Verse 22 says he finally realized it was the angel of the Lord. Confusing? Realization seems to come in stages.)

4. **Describe the first sign God gave Gideon.** (Fire came from the rock and consumed the sacrifice.)

Read Judges 6:36–40.

5. **What in this passage speaks to you about Gideon's doubts?** (Gideon had the nerve to begin with, "If you will save Israel" after God's promise in 6:14.)

6. **What in this passage speaks to you of God's patience?** (God outdid himself by providing a bowlful of dew; he wasn't put off or angry when the second test was requested.)

OPTION
Accountability Partners
Have accountability partners meet during the week to discuss their doubts and how God is dealing with their doubts. Have them also discuss how God is challenging them and ask them to pray for each other concerning doubts.

OPTION
Worship Ideas
Read Psalm 13:1–6 together as an act of worship.

OPTION
Memory Verse
"The Lord turned to him and said, 'Go in the strength you have and save Israel out of Midian's hand. Am I not sending you?'" (Judges 6:14).

Read Judges 7:1–8.

7. Less than 1 percent of the original number of fighting men were left after God urged Gideon to let the others go. How could they expect to win with this type of "military downsizing"?

8. OPTION: **Based on anything you remember about how Israel came to possess the Promised Land, why did it make sense that Gideon was allowed to use only less than 1 percent of his original army?** (God often used dramatic means to prove that he was the reason Israel overcame. For example, from last week's session, the walls of Jericho fell not by human might, but by God's might alone.)

Read Judges 7:9–15.

9. What evidence do we have that God saw into Gideon's heart and met his need? (In verse 10, God said, "If you are afraid, . . ." and Gideon apparently was.)

10. How did God use Gideon's enemies to minister to him?

TAKING THE NEXT STEP

Read the second paragraph of <u>Resource Sheet 2B</u>, "What Does God Do with Doubters?" and ask the following questions.

1. In what areas do you think your faith is only in the "kite string" phase? Feeling God has abandoned you (as Gideon did)? Intellectual doubt?

OPTION: If you wish, bring kite string and show that although it is not as sturdy as a bridge, it is difficult to break. It's a good start.

2. What kinds of things help assuage doubt and move faith into the "rope" and "cable" phases?

3. Who are the people in your life who are standing at either end of the chasm feeding the rope and cable—helping you overcome doubt?

Tour Map Through Gideon's Doubts

SCENE 1: GIDEON AND THE ANGEL OF THE LORD
Judges 6:11–23

Gideon's Doubts:

God's Response:

(In verses 24–35, God asked Gideon to tear down the altar to Baal, chop down the Asherah pole [equivalent to setting fire to the most popular X-rated theater in town], and use the Asherah pole wood to offer a burnt offering to God. Gideon did so—at night, because he was afraid—and the men of the town came to kill him. Gideon's father challenged them, however, to let Baal—if he was a god—take revenge on Gideon himself. They did so.)

SCENE 2: GIDEON WANTS ANOTHER SIGN
Judges 6:36–40

Gideon's Doubts:

God's Response:

SCENE 3: FROM 32,000 MEN TO 300 MEN
Judges 7:1–8

God's Challenge:

Gideon's Response:

SCENE 4: GOD GIVES GIDEON ONE MORE SIGN
Judges 7:9–15

Gideon's Fears:

God's Response:

RESULT: God gave Gideon and his army victory over their oppressors, the Midianites (Judges 7:16–25).

What Does God Do with Doubters?

1. Patience with the Honest Doubter

God was patient with Gideon, saying to him, "I will wait until you return" (Judges 6:18), and then showing him four dramatic signs that he was truly leading Gideon to victory. *We sometimes falsely imagine God as someone who is standing by ready to condemn us the first time we doubt his word.* But one of God's characteristics is patience. When we have honest doubts driven by our difficult circumstances or our desire to know the truth, God is patient with us.

2. Salvation for the Obedient Believer

Many of us believe, but we need help with our unbelief. A bridge was once built with a kite string. A construction worker flew a kite across the chasm to someone waiting on the other side. A rope was then attached to the kite string and pulled across the chasm. Then a cable was attached to the rope, then a series of cables and so on. Eventually a sturdy bridge was built that began with a kite string. Occasionally you may feel like your faith is nothing more than a kite string. But Jesus said if we had even the smallest amount of true faith—faith as small as a mustard seed—we could move mountains.

3. Evidence for the Sincere Seeker

Gideon put his faith in God, but God was patient enough to give Gideon evidences upon which to base that faith. Four times God showed Gideon dramatic signs that indicated he would give him the victory—the miraculous fire that burned up the offering, the two fleece incidents, and the dream of the Midianite.

God has given us the evidence of creation, the resurrection, and the Bible to reassure our faith in him. We can witness the changed lives of Christians throughout history as further evidence of God's truth. God will show evidence of his truth to the sincere seeker.

4. Victory to the Faithful

"During that night the Lord said to Gideon, 'Get up, go down against the camp, because I am going to give it into your hands'" (Judges 7:9). When we doubt, God is going to demand that we take a step of faith and act obediently anyway. Someone said, "Faith is going to the edge of all the light you have and then taking one more step." God gives a lot of light, and Gideon finally took that step of faith God required by gathering his men and facing the enemy.

—Adapted from *Life Preservers,* by Bob Russell

Tell Me a Story

Plan a story about fictional character Dan or Ann and his or her interaction with God. You don't have to write out the entire story. Just jot down a few notes. The general plan should be:

SCENE 1:

Dan/Ann expresses doubt about one of these things, which are indeed God's will:
- Did God really choose me to do this certain task?
- Is God really leading me to do a certain thing?
- Does God really want me to use this method that doesn't look practical or reasonable?

Possible areas of doubts: health, work, family, resolving problems, prayer life

God responds. (This is fiction, so don't worry about being far-fetched. If you like, let God speak aloud to Dan/Ann as he did to Gideon.)

SCENE 2:

God challenges Dan/Ann to behave in a godly way that requires faith.

Dan/Ann follows through. (Let him/her falter a little, if you want.)

SCENE 3:

Dan/Ann expresses doubt.

God reassures Dan/Ann in some way.

SCENE 4:

Dan/Ann follows through in obedience.

Doubting Styles...

Recurring thoughts about (pick one):
- ❏ going as a missionary to an Islamic country in which Christianity is prohibited
- ❏ cleaning up the church nursery so visitors would be more willing to leave their kids there
- ❏ mowing your neighbor's lawn when you mow yours
- ❏ volunteering at a soup kitchen
- ❏ other:

TELL ME MORE

I'M WILLING TO PONDER IT

TELL ME MORE
(I'm Just Saying That—
I Don't Mean It)

HEAVY-DUTY DOUBTER

Three

God's Promises in Times of Loneliness

Studies have revealed the following statistics about loneliness:
- Fifteen percent of people feel lonely most or all of the time.
- Seventy-eight percent feel lonely at least some of the time.
- Twenty percent of all households in America consist of a person living alone (a 385 percent increase over 30 years ago).

Two common reasons for loneliness are:

Failure: You are tempted to believe you have let people down, that you are worthless, that no one would want to befriend someone who has failed.

Isolation: You can feel isolated and be surrounded by people. The most lonely experience I ever had was my first year in college—400 miles from home with no prospect of returning for two months. That first week I stared in the darkness alone, unable to sleep. For several weeks I would listen to the broadcast of the Pittsburgh Pirates baseball games through the static, just to get some feel for home.

—Adapted from *Life Preservers,* by Bob Russell

Central Theme	God responds to times of loneliness and meets our needs as we learn to trust him, get involved in life, and be patient.
Lesson Aim	Group members will discover biblical principles for responding to loneliness and discuss how they can be put into practice.
Bible Background	Ruth 1:15–19; 2:5–20; 3:7–13; 4:9, 10
For Further Study	Read Chapter 3 of *Life Preservers.*

Classes

Materials You'll Need For This Session

Resource Sheets 3A and 3B, Transparency 3A, pens or pencils, chalk and chalkboard

BUILDING COMMUNITY

Display <u>Transparency 3A</u>, "When It Feels as if It's Only Me, Myself, and I." Ask class members to suggest reasons for loneliness. Get them started with reasons suggested in the introduction—failure and isolation. Write their ideas on the left or right side of the cartoon. You may need the space at the bottom later in the lesson.

Cartoon Talkback
5–10 Minutes

If the above seems too heavy a way to begin, display the transparency and ask class members to tell about a time they were homesick. Have a story of your own ready.

OPTION
A Lighter Touch
5–10 Minutes

Write these two words on the chalkboard: *alone, loneliness.* Ask class members, **What's the difference between these two things?** After they answer, ask, **How can someone be alone, yet not be lonely?**

OPTION
Definitions
3–5 Minutes

CONSIDERING SCRIPTURE

Distribute copies of <u>Resource Sheet 3A</u>, "Interviewing Ruth," and ask class members to form groups of three or four. Have them work together to come up with answers Ruth might give if she were interviewed on a television talk show. After they're finished, ask a few groups to read their responses to Question 1. Continue that way for the other two questions. If any of the following ideas were left out, you may wish to add them.

Interview
10–15 Minutes

1. Why were you so stubborn? In her time of need, Ruth chose the companionship of Naomi as well as the comfort of God. She was from a pagan culture, but she saw the truth of Jehovah God and believed in him, which enabled him to help her more.

2. What did you do to keep yourself busy and useful? She gleaned in the fields—back-breaking and tiresome work in the Palestinian heat.

3. What did you do instead of chasing Boaz? She worked patiently in his field and established herself as a woman of noble character. She didn't chase men. Even when she ate with Boaz (2:14), she refrained from pushing herself forward. She may not, however, have realized that Boaz was her kinsman-redeemer.

OPTION
Acting Out Interview
3–5 Minutes

After class members have done their work to complete the interview, ask two volunteers from several groups to "perform" their interviews. One can play the interviewer and the other can play Ruth.

OPTION
Cartoon Talkback
15 Minutes

Display again <u>Transparency 3A</u>. Explain that Ruth's situation as described in today's lesson passage must have left her feeling much like this cartoon. Ask that as a volunteer reads this passage, class members consider what Ruth did (either intentionally or unintentionally) that kept her from feeling so lonely. After the passage is read, write class members' suggestions on the transparency under the cartoon.

TAKING THE NEXT STEP

Resource Sheet Survey
5 Minutes

Distribute copies of <u>Resource Sheet 3B</u>, and ask a volunteer to read it. Ask class members, **What other means, besides those mentioned on this sheet, does God use to assuage loneliness?** (Another means not mentioned is friendship. Ruth's attachment to her mother-in-law provided that.) Survey the class by asking for a show of hands and asking, **Which of the three suggestions on the sheet are you most likely to follow when you become lonely?** (Call out each one and get a count.) **Which one are you least likely to follow?** After you find out which one is used least, ask these two questions: **Why is it so difficult to do this? How can we help ourselves make it easier to do this?**

Case Studies
10–15 Minutes

Distribute copies of <u>Resource Sheet 3B</u>, "God's Responses to Loneliness," if you haven't already, and ask class members to consider these points in light of the following case studies. Read each case study one at a time and ask, **What would you suggest to each of these people?**
MARRIED WOMAN: You have just moved to another town after having many friends in your own town. You've joined a church, but you haven't made any friends there. You're thinking about changing churches to see if you might make more friends elsewhere.
OLDER WOMAN: You have to move in with your son's active family. You have your own room, but you feel lost and overwhelmed. So much activity. The kitchen isn't yours to do as you please. You know you're in the way.
SINGLE GUY: Your wife has just left you. Every woman at the office is throwing herself at you. What do you do to get through this?

OPTION
Group Case Studies
5–10 Minutes

If you're pressed for time, have the class form groups and read one of the case studies to each group. Ask them to look over <u>Resource Sheet 3B</u> for ideas.

Groups

BUILDING COMMUNITY

1. What is your favorite song with the word *lonely* in it?

2. OPTION (holding up Transparency 3A): **When have you felt this way?**

3. What has been the greatest help to you when you've felt this way?

CONSIDERING SCRIPTURE

Introduce this passage by explaining that Ruth was a woman of Moab who married an Israelite man. Her husband died, as did her brother-in-law and father-in-law. When her mother-in-law Naomi wanted to return to Israel, Ruth persuaded her to let her come along.

Read Ruth 1:15–19.

1. How would you describe Ruth's attachment to the Moabite religion (which didn't believe in Jehovah God)?

2. Both grief and changing cultures are stressful events. Why do you think Ruth chose to leave behind her homeland in her time of grief? (She seemed linked to Naomi in a special way, perhaps protective of her. Or she may have loved the Israelite way, especially God. She must have been quite independent.)

Read Ruth 2:5–20.

3. What about Ruth seemed to impress Boaz? (She worked steadily, v. 7; she helped her mother-in-law, v. 11.)

4. What help did Boaz offer?

5. What further evidence does this passage provide that Ruth was a hard worker? (She gleaned until evening and then threshed the grain.)

Materials You'll Need For This Session

Transparency 3A (make a photocopy on paper to hold up to the group) Resource Sheet 3B

OPTION
Accountability Partners
Have partners meet and discuss situations in which they feel lonely, perhaps due to failure or isolation. Ask them also to review Resource Sheet 3B and consider ways that God is helping them fill that loneliness.

OPTION
Worship Ideas
Read Psalm 25 together as an act of worship. (Be sure to include verse 16.)

OPTION
Memory Verse
"But Ruth replied, 'Don't urge me to leave you or to turn back from you. Where you go I will go, and where you stay I will stay. Your people will be my people and your God my God. Where you die I will die, and there I will be buried. May the Lord deal with me, be it ever so severely, if anything but death separates you and me'" (Ruth 1:16, 17).

6. How did Ruth find out Boaz was one of her kinsman-redeemers?

Read Ruth 3:7–13; 4:9, 10.

7. Based on the context, what would you guess Ruth's lying at the feet of Boaz meant? (She followed the Israelite custom for a servant to lay at her master's feet. This was to inform him that he was her kinsman-redeemer and could find someone to marry her, or marry her himself.)

8. What did Boaz find in Ruth that was admirable?

9. OPTION: Distribute copies of Resource Sheet 3B, "God's Responses to Loneliness." **How would you answer someone who says that Ruth's story is one of a widow trying to catch a man to fill her loneliness?**

TAKING THE NEXT STEP

1. In what ways has God been a comfort to you in lonely times?

2. How has it helped you to get involved (or work hard) as Ruth did?

3. What can we do to help ourselves be more patient to wait through times of loneliness?

Interviewing Ruth

I understand that you were very lonely. You lived in Moab with your husband, your husband's brother and wife, your husband's father and wife. Then, all three of the men died. You and your sister-in-law wanted to come with Naomi, your mother-in-law, but she resisted. Finally, your sister-in-law gave in, but you didn't.

1. Why were you so stubborn? (See Ruth 1:15–19.)

2. A lot of people have trouble focusing and getting involved when they're in a new place. What did you do to keep yourself busy and useful? (See Ruth 2:5–9.)

3. You could have approached Boaz immediately since he was one of your kinsmen-redeemers (the closest relative of a deceased person responsible for caring for a widow). What did you do instead? (See Ruth 2:10–20; 3:7–13; 4:9, 10.)

God's Responses To Loneliness

1. God will comfort you if you TRUST IN HIM (Ruth 1:15–19).

Ruth made the right decision to follow Jehovah. Her Moabite gods couldn't have brought her comfort. Others today turn to alcohol or drugs or to a false religion rather than depending on the Lord and waiting for him to cure their loneliness.

2. God will bless you if you GET INVOLVED and WORK HARD (Ruth 2:5–9).

Ruth could have moped around her new home in Judah, allowing others to feel sorry for her, demanding that others take care of her, and praying that God would lead her to a new husband. Instead Ruth worked hard, not only for herself, but for her mother-in-law. Ruth went to work picking up the leftover grain in the fields. The welfare system of that day required that the reapers not harvest a field a second time, but leave the leftovers for the poor.

Hard work cures loneliness by filling time, giving us a sense of self-worth, and helping us gain the respect of others. There is no better cure for loneliness or depression than doing something good for somebody else.

3. God will guide you if you are PATIENT (Ruth 2:10–20; 3:7–13; 4:9, 10).

Ruth's heart must have raced as she sat across the dinner table from this wealthy man, Boaz, her kinsman-redeemer, wondering if God were providing a cure for her loneliness! But Ruth did not lose patience. She continued to work hard and care for her mother-in-law Naomi, waiting for the Lord's timing.

You have probably witnessed someone make a terrible mistake because he or she was not patient during a time of loneliness. Single people will compromise their convictions for a one-night stand rather than wait till they find someone who will stay faithful to them for life. Others marry too quickly after a divorce, only to wake up several months later with someone they really do not know.

◆　　◆　　◆　　◆　　◆

A pastor told about visiting an old Indian squaw who lived alone in a rugged log cabin. She was sitting in her rocker on the front porch when he drove up. He got out of the car and called, "Are you all alone, ma'am?"

"Well, son," she responded. "It's just me and Jesus!"

If the Lord is our companion, we need never feel lonely, even when we are alone.

—Adapted from *Life Preservers,* by Bob Russell

When It Feels as if It's Only
Me
and I *Myself*

Four

God's Promises in Times of Financial Stress

*I*t probably would not surprise you to learn that most Americans have trouble with money. Here are some statistics.

• Four out of five Americans owe more than they own.
• Forty percent of Americans borrow more than they can make monthly payments on.
• Eighty-five out of one hundred Americans have less than $250 in cash saved by age 65 (according to Social Security statistics).
• The average American gives less than 2 percent to charitable institutions. The average church member gives 2.5 percent.
• Approximately 50 percent of all divorces are caused by or related to financial pressures in the home.

It's no wonder Jesus had so much to say about money. Sixteen of his thirty-eight parables were about money matters. Jesus spoke about stewardship more than he spoke about Heaven or Hell. He talked about money five times more than he talked about prayer.

—Adapted from *Life Preservers,* by Bob Russell

Central Theme	God promises to provide basic necessities to those who are faithful.
Lesson Aim	Group members will examine what God promises during times of financial stress, and consider how they need to adjust their attitudes toward money.
Bible Background	1 Kings 17:1–6, various Scripture verses about money
For Further Study	Read Chapter 4 of *Life Preservers.*

*C*lasses

BUILDING COMMUNITY

Display <u>Transparency 4A</u>, "Money Troubles," and ask
class members to help you compose a limerick with the
first lines already in place. (Usually the first, second, and last
lines of a limerick rhyme with each other, and the third and
fourth lines rhyme with each other.) Money is often an uncomfortable topic, especially at church, so use this activity to introduce this topic in a fun way.

Have class members form pairs or groups and work on
the limericks individually. Ask several to share their limericks and write them on the transparency for everyone to read.

Read aloud to the class the statistics listed behind bullets
in the introduction, and ask class members, **Which ones
do you think are false?** Listen carefully to their answers and
then tell the class that all the statements are true.

CONSIDERING SCRIPTURE

Ask class members to turn to *1 Kings 17* and have a volunteer read *17:1–6*. Summarize: **In Elijah's work as a
prophet, he predicted a drought in Israel and then he had to
figure out how to survive it himself. He ended up living in the
Kerith Ravine.**

Then distribute copies of <u>Resource Sheet 4A</u>, "So, This Is My
Reward?" Explain further that Elijah continued to be both obedient and dynamic by:
- bringing the son of the widow of Zarephath back to life
  (1 Kings 17:7–24)
- conducting a contest between God and Baal on Mt. Carmel
  in which fire consumed God's sacrifice and the prophets of
  Baal were defeated (1 Kings 18)
- condemning wicked King Ahab publicly (1 Kings 21)

Then ask this question: **What does this tell us about the so-
called health and wealth philosophy, that when you obey God,
God blesses you?** (Bob Russell described it this way: "Tammy
Faye Bakker used to say, 'If you pray for a new car, make sure to
tell God what color you want, because you are going to get it!'")

Limerick Writing
5 Minutes

OPTION
Group Limerick Writing
5 Minutes

OPTION
True False Quiz Hoax
5 Minutes

OPTION: (for introducing
Scripture)
Can of Worms Question
5–10 Minutes

Materials You'll Need For This Session

Resource Sheets
4A–4C, Transparency
4A, pens or pencils,
colored pens (op-
tional), chalk and
chalkboard

Journal Entry
5–10 Minutes

☐ Have a volunteer read *1 Kings 17:1–6*, if you didn't use the previous "Can of Worms" step. Distribute copies of Resource Sheet 4B, "Elijah's Prayer Journal." Say, **Imagine for a moment that you are Elijah** (keeping in mind anything you may have read on Resource Sheet 4A). **Complete Elijah's prayer journal by finishing the sentences on the top portion of the page. Feel free to make requests of God and ask God questions. Don't be afraid of being candid about lack of money.** (The lower portion of the page is to be used later.)

Matching
5–10 Minutes

☐ To look at specific Scriptures about the financial resources God promises to give to the faithful, have class members look at Resource Sheet 4C, "What God Says About Money." The Scriptures on the right do not correlate with the principles on the left, so ask them to match the correct reference with each principle. Suggested answers are: 1–d, 2–g, 3–a, 4–h, 5–c, 6–f, 7–e, 8–b.

If you used the "Can of Worms" activity, above, you may wish to ask, **How does this shed light on the idea that God makes sure that believers have the money they want?** (Jesus had little wealth and God promises believers about the same—only basic provisions. The one who tithed received special blessings according to Old Testament Law.)

TAKING THE NEXT STEP

Transition Question
3–5 Minutes

☐ Read the following story:

My friend told me about getting a new sports car. In his youth he had dreamed of owning a Corvette, but he became a school teacher so his chances were slim. However, he was single for a long time, so he had the chance to save up and finally bought a beautiful metallic blue Corvette.

The first couple of weeks he loved it. But then he grew tired of hearing remarks like, "We must be paying school-teachers too much these days." He worried about getting it scratched, so he would take up two spaces in the parking lot. When he returned, he would find nasty notes on the windshield. He discovered the police were more likely to stop a Corvette because they automatically suspected him of speeding. He worried about someone stealing the car, so he had a theft alarm put in it. Then it would go off in the middle of the night and wake up half the apartment complex. After a few months, he was glad to get rid of it. (Adapted from *Life Preservers*, by Bob Russell.)

Ask, **How does this story show that God's provision of basic necessities is wiser than our desire for luxuries?**

If you didn't distribute copies of <u>Resource Sheet 4B</u>, "Elijah's Prayer Journal," earlier, do so now. Direct class members' attention to the lower portion of the page and say, **Write your own prayer, and don't be afraid to be as honest as Elijah probably was. You can use the first few sentence starters if you wish, or write your own. When you get to the last sentence, try to fill it in with a principle from Resource Sheet 4C.** (Distribute copies of <u>Resource Sheet 4C</u>, if you haven't already used it.)

Have class members look at their photocopies of <u>Resource Sheet 4C</u>, "What God Says About Money." Make colored pens available and encourage them to circle or color in the following way:

FIND THE SCRIPTURAL PRINCIPLE OR REFERENCE:	COLOR IT WITH THE PEN AVAILABLE THAT IS:
they have put into use most often	their favorite color
they have most neglected	their least favorite color
they believe God would most like for them to incorporate in their attitude or habits	the color they are most comfortable with

Personal Prayer Journal Writing
5–10 Minutes

OPTION
Color Coding
3–5 Minutes

Groups

BUILDING COMMUNITY

1. Do you agree or disagree with this statement? God promises only to provide basic necessities in life. Ask respondents why they answered as they did. (This can be interpreted several ways. The purpose is to generate discussion, so don't offer conclusions.) End the discussion with, **Let's look at the experience of one of God's servants.**

2. OPTION: **What ideas about God and money have you heard that are clearly wrong?**

3. OPTION: **The average American family is three weeks away from bankruptcy. How do you think God views this financial stress in the larger scheme of things?**

CONSIDERING SCRIPTURE

Read 1 Kings 17:1–6.

1. Why do you think Elijah's drought prediction would have upset Israel's wicked King Ahab? (This highly agrarian culture used a lot of water. It was also a sign of God's judgment on the king.)

2. Why do you think the Lord ordered Elijah to the brook? (Probably for his safety from Ahab, who would later try to kill him. Also, perhaps to teach Elijah to depend on God.)

3. Imagine a canyon or ravine near your home or that was near your home as a child. How would you like living there?

4. OPTION: Distribute copies of Resource Sheet 4A, "So This Is My Reward?" **How does this information color what otherwise sounds like an idyllic life in a ravine?**

Distribute copies of Resource Sheet 4C, "What God Says About Money," and ask volunteers to read the verses on the right. Or, have class members look up the following and read them aloud: *Malachi 3:10–12, Matthew 6:28–30; 19:29.*

> ### Materials You'll Need For This Session
>
> Resource Sheets 4A (optional) and 4C

5. What basic provisions does God promise to provide? (Matthew 6:28–30).

6. What did God promise in the Old Testament to those who tithe? (Malachi 3:10–12).

7. What does God promise to those who give sacrificially? (Matthew 19:29).

TAKING THE NEXT STEP

1. How do you feel about God's promise to provide only basic necessities for believers?
❑ disappointed—I've learned to want more.
❑ stunned—I didn't realize I expected so much from God.
❑ satisfied—many of the world's people struggle to even achieve that. I see I am blessed.

2. How does understanding God's provision of simple things reflect on the financial stresses people have in our times?

3. OPTION: Malachi 3:10 ("'Test me in this,' says the Lord Almighty, 'and see if I will not throw open the floodgates of heaven and pour out so much blessing that you will not have room enough for it.'") **tempts us to "give to get." What is the problem with that attitude?**

So, This Is My Reward?

In 1 Kings 17, Elijah the Tishbite was called upon to be the mouth of God during the reign of Ahab, one of the most wicked rulers in the history of Israel. You would think that God would reward Elijah for his boldness before the king. Surely Elijah would not be made to suffer from the famine that came as a result of God's judgment. Surely he was allowed to go to a foreign country that was not under such judgment and feast like a king.

Yet, for his faithfulness, Elijah was called to hide out in a ravine, drink the water there (until it later dried up), and be fed by ravens! Those were not exactly enviable accommodations! As the brook began to dry up, the water probably became warm, stagnant, and full of algae.

Ravens were not ideal waiters, either. They brought him bread and meat in the morning and evening. That may not sound too bad unless you know something about ravens. The Israelites were not allowed to eat ravens "because they are detestable" (Leviticus 11:13–15). Gary Richmond, a former zookeeper, explained:

> Ravens are scavengers, therefore they and anything they touch are also unclean. They'll eat just about anything, dead and decaying meat, rodents, insects, and rotten garbage. They are without taste and are absolutely disgusting. If that weren't enough, it was a well-known fact that ravens store their food in cow dung to prevent it from freezing in the winter. They also sift through the cow dung searching for tasty dung beetles.

> I'm absolutely sure that Elijah's stomach turned when the first delivery raven arrived. Knowing their habits, he would have wondered where the raven's beak had been just prior to its visit with the food. He may also have known that ravens have an interesting relationship with wolves. Some people believe that ravens have a way of communicating the whereabouts of live food to wolves. Then the ravens get to eat the wolves' leftovers, which generally is a favorite food of theirs anyway (Gary Richmond, *All God's Creatures: Spiritual Lessons from Animals of the Bible*, Word, Inc. 1991, p. 164).

—Adapted from *Life Preservers*, by Bob Russell

Elijah's Prayer Journal

Dear God,

About these ravens . . .

How long . . .

Have you noticed that the water is . . .

Waiting to hear from you,

Elijah

My Prayer Journal

Dear God,

About . . .

How long . . .

Have you noticed . . .

The scriptural principle that's toughest for me is:

Help me meditate on this and come to practice it in my life.

Signed,

What God Says About Money

1. Jesus' wealth

a. "For we brought nothing into the world, and we can take nothing out of it. But if we have food and clothing, we will be content with that" (1 Timothy 6:7, 8).

2. God promises freedom from worry

b. "And why do you worry about clothes? See how the lilies of the field grow. They do not labor or spin. Yet I tell you that not even Solomon in all his splendor was dressed like one of these. If that is how God clothes the grass of the field, which is here today and tomorrow is thrown into the fire, will he not much more clothe you, O you of little faith?" (Matthew 6:28–30).

3. The importance of appropriate expectations

c. "'Bring the whole tithe into the storehouse, that there may be food in my house. Test me in this,' says the Lord Almighty, 'and see if I will not throw open the floodgates of heaven and pour out so much blessing that you will not have room enough for it. I will prevent pests from devouring your crops, and the vines in your fields will not cast their fruit,' says the Lord Almighty. 'Then all the nations will call you blessed, for yours will be a delightful land,' says the Lord Almighty" (Malachi 3:10–12).

4. Eagerness for money ruins you

d. "Foxes have holes and birds of the air have nests, but the Son of Man has no place to lay his head" (Matthew 8:20).

5. God gave special blessings to the one who tithed

e. "And everyone who has left houses or brothers or sisters or father or mother or children or fields for my sake will receive a hundred times as much and will inherit eternal life" (Matthew 19:29).

6. Be generous with those in the world without riches

f. "Command those who are rich in this present world not to be arrogant nor to put their hope in wealth, which is so uncertain, but to put their hope in God, who richly provides us with everything for our enjoyment. Command them to do good, to be rich in good deeds, and to be generous and willing to share" (1 Timothy 6:17, 18).

7. God gives special spiritual blessings to the sacrificial giver

g. "I am not saying this because I am in need, for I have learned to be content whatever the circumstances. I know what it is to be in need, and I know what it is to have plenty. I have learned the secret of being content in any and every situation, whether well fed or hungry, whether living in plenty or in want" (Philippians 4:11, 12).

8. God promises believers basic provisions

h. "For the love of money is a root of all kinds of evil. Some people, eager for money, have wandered from the faith and pierced themselves with many griefs" (1 Timothy 6:10).

Money Troubles

1

There once was a man with no money

He _____

_____

_____

_____

2

There once a woman who loved money

She _____

_____

_____

_____

CLUES: Possible rhymes with money (you can add your own): funny, honey, bunny, runny, sunny.

Five

God's Promises in Times of Temptation

A pseudopious Christian boasted, "I never encounter the devil!" But a wise saint responded, "That is understandable. Two people going down the same path in the same direction seldom bump into one another."

God does not promise to exempt us from temptations. If you are going in the opposite direction of Satan, you will meet him coming toward you.

Most of the time people rationalize that their sin really isn't so bad. One woman said her bad temper really was no big deal; it was like dynamite—she would blow up for a second, then it was all over. But whom did she hurt in the process?

God's promises are both challenging and comforting. Temptation can be overcome with the help of God. That is comforting; it is also challenging because it removes all excuses.

—Adapted from *Life Preservers,* by Bob Russell

Central Theme	It's wise to stay focused on God rather than flirting with temptation, which can bring shame and disaster.
Lesson Aim	Group members will examine the consequences of trying to serve God and flirt with temptation and consider what is needed to avoid this destructive behavior.
Bible Background	Numbers 22:1–38; 1 Corinthians 10:13
For Further Study	Read Chapter 5 of *Life Preservers.*

PLAN ONE

*C*lasses

BUILDING COMMUNITY

Bring several paper cups (plastic foam or wax is fine). Put water or coffee in the first one and explain, **A good cup is useful. It has sides and a bottom and it holds liquid.** Then pour some liquid into a cup that you poked a tiny hole in. (Place another cup or paper towel under it to catch the liquid.) **It doesn't matter how tiny the hole is—the cup will not work properly.**

Compare the cups to Christian behavior: **The cup without a hole is like a Christian who is focused on God and stays away from temptation. The other cup is like those Christians who want to focus on God, but their strength is limited because they flirt with temptation. We think flirting with temptation isn't crucial because we're not exactly giving in (just like saying, "It's only a small hole"), but it puts us in a dangerous, vulnerable position.**

Write this on the chalkboard: "Trying to serve God while flirting with temptation is like . . ." Ask class members to come up with a comparison similar to this one: ". . . like trying to drive both ways on a two-way street."

CONSIDERING SCRIPTURE

Distribute copies of Resource Sheet 5A, "Balaam's Attitude Check," and explain that the class is going to rate Balaam's attitude and behavior in the passages listed. Start by having a volunteer read *Numbers 22:1–8*. Then ask, **By the time we get to what's happening in verse 8, how would you rate Balaam's attitude on this chart?**

Opinions will vary. Balaam could have been flirting with temptation because he considered putting a curse on Israel. But then his entire occupation—sorcery—was full of temptation, so some might think he had dived into temptation long before that time.

Ask class members to mark the sheet this way: **If you think Balaam was escaping temptation, place a dot in the center of the square in the top row and first column. If you think he was flirting with temptation, place a dot in the second row, first column. If you think he was diving into temptation, place a dot in the bottom row, first column.**

Object Lesson
5 Minutes

> **Materials You'll Need For This Session**
>
> Resource Sheets 5A and 5B, Transparency 5A, three paper cups, pens or pencils, chalk and chalkboard

OPTION
Fun Comparisons
5 Minutes

Attitude Graph
10–15 Minutes

Do the same with each passage listed at the bottom of the chart. Below are thoughts to bring up for each column. Let class members decide categories for themselves.

Verses 9–13: It could be argued that he was "diving into temptation" because he asked God to do something as mean-spirited as curse a nation. On the other hand, he did obey God (v. 13), which would indicate "flirting with temptation."

Verses 14–18: Balaam stood firm against temptation, escaping it.

Verse 19: Balaam hedged, evidenced by how he was willing to ask God again. He was probably flirting with temptation.

Verses 20–30: By this time, he was so deafened by temptation (due perhaps to money, fame, or prestige) that he was less able to hear God than his donkey. This rests on the border of flirting with temptation and diving into it.

Verses 31–40: Balaam was convinced by the angel and obeyed God's orders. He escaped temptation.

After class members have marked their dots in the squares, have them connect the dots to form a graph of the ups and downs of Balaam's attitude.

OPTION
Clapping Meter
10–15 Minutes

Instead of using the chart on <u>Resource Sheet 5A</u>, write the categories on the chalkboard and ask class members to express their opinion through loudness of clapping. For example, after Numbers 22:1–8 is read and discussed, ask those who think Balaam escaped temptation to clap their hands; then ask those who think he flirted with temptation to clap; finally, ask those who think he dived into temptation to clap. When the class is done with the exercise, they won't have a chart, but they'll have a better sense of how others responded to Balaam's behavior.

OPTION
Digging Deeper
5 Minutes

If class members need further clarification about why Balaam's behavior was so sinful that an angel of the Lord would appear and nearly kill him, distribute copies of <u>Resource Sheet 5B</u>, "Unraveling Balaam's Story." After having someone read the first section aloud, ask a class member to summarize where Balaam went wrong.

Then have someone read aloud section two, "How Did Balaam Turn Out?" Ask, **What are the consequences of trying to serve God while flirting with temptation?** (Flirting with temptation creates turmoil. Pondering temptation can cloud your judgment, so you have to keep examining motives for purity.)

Have someone read *1 Corinthians 10:13*. Ask, **If Balaam had sought the "way of escape" or "way out" mentioned in 1 Corinthians 10:13, what might he have done?**

If you think class members aren't catching the difference between escaping temptation and flirting with it, read the third and fourth paragraphs (italicized) from Resource Sheet 5B about the preacher and the donuts. Say, **Driving past the donut shop numerous times is flirting with temptation. How could the preacher have anticipated this possible temptation and sought to escape it?**

OPTION
Illustration
5 Minutes

TAKING THE NEXT STEP

Before class, read the case studies at the bottom of Transparency 5A, "Staying Focused on God," and prayerfully consider which ones to use with your class. Circle them or mark them on the transparency. In class, display the transparency and ask class members, **How would the person in each case study behave if he or she wished to flirt with temptation? If he or she wished to escape temptation?**

Case Study Continuum
15 Minutes

Ask class members to silently consider a temptation present in their lives. Then ask them to focus prayerfully on the "Flirt with Temptation" side of the continuum. Ask, **If you were to flirt with that temptation, how would you behave?** Give them a few minutes. Then ask them to focus on the other side. Ask, **If you were to proactively seek escape from the temptation, how would you behave?**

OPTION
Personalizing the Continuum
5–10 Minutes

*G*roups

BUILDING COMMUNITY

1. Ask class members to paraphrase this familiar saying: "All the things I really like to do are either _____, _____, or _____." (Alexander Wollcott said, "illegal, immoral, or fattening."

2. OPTION: **Look through your wallet and pick out an item that represents a temptation to you. (For example, a credit card presents the temptation of overspending. A picture of your kids might represent the temptation to neglect them or smother them.)**

CONSIDERING SCRIPTURE

Read Numbers 22:1–20.

Explain that the Israelites are in the process of going to the Promised Land.

1. What do Balak's actions tell you about the general character of the Moabites as a nation? (They didn't trust God to the point that they hired a sorcerer to attack the Israelites.)

2. What did Balak do to entice Balaam to come with him?

3. What else might have made Balaam want to go with Balak? (Being part of the Moabite "in crowd"; being prestigious and important to a king)

4. What shift occurred in Balaam's thinking from verse 18 to verse 19? (He decided to go back and consult with God again. Perhaps he thought that nagging might change God's mind.)

Read Numbers 22:21–41.

5. How could God have been "very angry" that Balaam went (v. 22) when God had told Balaam to go (v. 20)? (Distribute copies of Resource Sheet 5B, "Unraveling Balaam's Story," to help explain this.)

6. Why do you think the angel of the Lord rebuked Balaam for beating his donkey when the problem centered around his flirting with the temptation to curse Israel? (Various answers are possible. One is that his hardheartedness to his donkey showed that he was not open to what she might be saying to him. His single focus was on meeting Balak and trying to manipulate God into doing Balak's will.)

7. How obedient was Balaam when all was said and done? (He didn't curse Israel, either in this chapter or the next. New Testament comments, however, indicate that his flirting with temptation led him to disaster.)

Have someone read 1 Corinthians 10:13.

8. If Balaam had sought the "way of escape" or "way out" mentioned in 1 Corinthians 10:13, what do you think he might have done?

9. Even though Balaam ultimately obeyed God in this situation, where did he go wrong?

TAKING THE NEXT STEP

1. In what situations do we commonly flirt with temptation while trying to remain true to God in our lives?

2. What does this passage tell us about the consequences of flirting with temptations?

3. What attitude can keep us from flirting with temptation?

Balaam's Attitude Check

ESCAPING TEMPTATION						
FLIRTING WITH TEMPTATION						
DIVING INTO TEMPTATION						
NUMBERS 22:	1–8	9–13	14–18	19	20–30	31–40

Unraveling Balaam's Story

1. Where Did Balaam Go Wrong?

God told Balaam not to go with Balak, and he didn't (v. 12). Then God told Balaam he could go, and he did (v. 20). So, why did the angel of the Lord almost kill him?

Bob Russell explains, After his bold refusal (v. 18), Balaam added, "Now stay here tonight as the others did, and I will find out *what else* the Lord will tell me (v. 19, emphasis added). The Bible warns against giving the devil a "foothold" (Ephesians 4:27). Balaam had done just that. He knew what God wanted him to say, but he was flirting with temptation. "Riches are no temptation to me," Balaam boasted. "But stay the night, and let me try God again. Maybe he'll change his mind."

One overweight preacher announced to his staff that he was going on a diet, and then appeared the next day with a dozen donuts. His secretary said, "I thought you were on a diet."

"I was, but God wants me off it," the preacher explained. "I drove by the bakery and I prayed, 'Lord, if you don't want me to buy any donuts, don't allow there to be an open parking place in front of the bakery.' Wouldn't you know it! The eighth time I drove around the block there was a space right by the door! I figured it must be God's will."

Balaam was hoping God would change his mind, and it would be God's will for him to go with the king's men. He knew what God had said, but he could not resist the temptation. Balaam was growing too familiar with the idea of going with the princes, getting rich, and becoming famous.

Strangely, God came to Balaam and said, "Fine, go with the men" (v. 20, paraphrased). God will not take away our free will. If we continue to flirt with temptation, he will not keep us from committing the sin. But God was not happy with Balaam.

2. How Did Balaam Turn Out?

Balaam flirted with temptations of fame, peer pressure, and wealth, but God forgave him. Because Balaam turned and obeyed God, and spoke only the words God gave him, the Lord used him to speak mighty and powerful words to King Balak. Balaam refused to curse God's chosen people, so he was not very popular with the king. But he was obedient to God, at least for a time.

—Adapted from *Life Preservers*, by Bob Russell

LATER: Balaam did not curse Israel, which made Balak angry with him. Later, Balaam was killed when the Israelites fought Midian (Numbers 31:8). This is how the New Testament sums up Balaam's life:

- "They have left the straight way and wandered off to follow the way of Balaam son of Beor, who *loved the wages of wickedness*" (2 Peter 2:15, emphasis added).
- "Nevertheless, I have a few things against you: You have people there who hold to the teaching of Balaam, who *taught Balak* to entice the Israelites to sin by eating food sacrificed to idols and by committing sexual immorality" (Revelation 2:14, emphasis added).

Staying Focused on God

Consider the situations below. How would he or she behave if she were to:

**Flirt with
Temptation**

**Escape from
Temptation**

1. Steve, who is married, is having increasingly long conversations (but saying nothing inappropriate) with a woman friend.

2. Brenda is noticing how others pad their expense accounts.

3. Jake has begun writing down too much business mileage in case he decides he needs more deductions on his income tax.

4. Sheila has decided not to tell potential buyers of her car about the defect in the radiator unless they specifically ask about it.

5. David is investing tithe money in stocks so he can give more later.

6. Nancy is waiting for someone at church to bring up a certain person so she can pass on the negative information she has about that person. (Nancy figures that if she doesn't bring it up, it's not really gossip. If she's asked questions, she's only answering truthfully.)

7. Brad keeps a hidden stash of candy and another of liquor—just in case he needs it.

8. While cooking dinner, Denise rehearses what she'll say to a certain person at work if he ever yells at her again.

Six

God's Promises in Times of Rebellion

Perhaps you have been running from God, and this chapter caught your eye for a good reason. Maybe you are facing temptation right now and you must choose whether you will run to God or away from God.

Maybe you have been praying for a son, daughter, friend, or parent who has rebelled against God. Sometimes when loved ones rebel, we pray that God might protect them. We can see they are running down a dangerous path away from God, and we do not want them to suffer.

But God may have a different plan in mind. The rebellious person may need pain or conflict—maybe poverty, a broken relationship, loneliness, or physical hardship—to arouse him from his slumber. Maybe our prayer should be, "Lord, whatever it takes to bring him back to you, please do it. I want his soul to be saved."

Adapted from Life Preservers, by Bob Russell

Central Theme	God promises discipline for those who rebel and restoration for those who repent.
Lesson Aim	Group members will consider scriptural principles regarding rebellion and restoration and consider how they need to respond to the rebellion that affects their life.
Bible Background	Jonah 1–4
For Further Study	Read Chapter 6 of *Life Preservers*.

Classes

Materials You'll Need For This Session

Resource Sheets 6A and 6B, Transparency 6A, pens or pencils, chalk and chalkboard

BUILDING COMMUNITY

Draw three columns on the chalkboard. At the top of each column, draw a simple face (a circle with a smile, two slashes for eyes, and a dot for a nose). On the first, draw long hair and write, "young adult." On the second, draw hair trimmed to the head and write, "middle adult." At the top of the last column, simply write, "older adult." Explain, **Rebellion is usually associated with young adults, but it's actually common among all age groups. Help me come up with at least five ways people in each age group rebel.** Class members are free to yell out their answers along with which group it fits in.

Brainstorming
10 Minutes

Write the word *rebellion* on the chalkboard and say, **What one word fits with the idea of rebellion to you? Maybe it's what you rebel against—rules, authority—or maybe it's a type of person who rebels or rouses rebellion from others—teenagers or know-it-all bosses.** Class members should say the word that fits and doesn't take too long to think of. Give them a few minutes and then ask for their responses.

Word Association
5–8 Minutes

CONSIDERING SCRIPTURE

Have class members form groups of five or six, and distribute copies of <u>Resource Sheet 6A</u> to each class member. Explain, **Read each section of the resource sheet. As you read, keep this question in mind, How does God treat humans when they rebel?** (Write this question on the chalkboard.)

Circulate among groups to see if anyone has questions. After ten minutes, ask members to report their answers to the question. Their responses will likely be versions of these three ideas:

1. God disciplines those who rebel. If you declare yourself to be a child of God, you can expect God to treat you like one of his children. He doesn't shrink from disciplining his children, nor does he water down his commands.

2. God restores those who repent. God loves the sinner even more than he hates the sin. He promises that no matter how far you have run from him, he will restore you if you repent. The only time God is pictured as being in a hurry is in the prodigal son parable. He runs to forgive his rebellious child who repented.

Finding Principles
15 Minutes

3. God's restoration is complete and whole. It leads to increased responsibility in the kingdom. Jonah was restored, but he still had to go to Nineveh. Simon Peter was forgiven after denying Jesus, but then Jesus commanded Peter, "Feed my sheep" (John 21:17).

Option
Small Group Study
10 Minutes

Write the same question on the chalkboard (**How does God treat humans when they rebel?**), and distribute copies of Resource Sheet 6A. Present the same question as above, but have the class form four groups and assign each group one of the four chapters of Jonah to search for the answer to the question.

Option
Debunking Myths
5–10 Minutes

Display Transparency 6A, "Myths About Rebellion," and ask a volunteer to read Myth 1. Then ask the three questions at the top of the transparency about that myth. Use material from the "Finding Principles" activity above to guide this discussion.

Option
Lecture
10–15 Minutes

Use the main points from Resource Sheet 6A, "Jonah at a Glance," to build a short, five-minute lecture. Use the resource sheet as a handout to keep students' interest.

TAKING THE NEXT STEP

Case Study
10 Minutes

Distribute copies of Resource Sheet 6B, and have someone read the case study in the box. Then pose the question stated below the box and read the instructions concerning Point A. Ask for responses, some of which may include these:

Point A: God doesn't give people a second chance. His sin was too bad. His sin was too widely-known. His family would never forgive, much less love, him again. God could never forgive, much less love, him again. It was too humiliating to live with this—he needed to abandon his family, leave town, and start over or even kill himself.

Read the question regarding Point B and ask for responses.

Point B: For his family, friends, church members, and even himself, he could never be trusted. He didn't deserve restoration.

Option
Small Groups
10 Minutes

Have the class form small groups and answer the questions from the "Case Study" activity above. Allow time for them to report to the entire class.

Option
Prayer Writing
5 Minutes

Read aloud the third paragraph of the introduction to this session. Ask class members to use the back of one of the resource sheets to write a prayer concerning the rebellion of a relative, friend, or themselves. Repeat the one offered in the introduction: "Lord, whatever it takes to bring (this person or me) back to you, please do it." Allow them several minutes to complete it.

*G*roups

BUILDING COMMUNITY

1. At what point in life do you think most people rebel—especially against God?

2. What usually keeps the rebel from coming back to God?

CONSIDERING SCRIPTURE

Read Jonah 1:1–10.

1. Why might Jonah have refused to preach to the Assyrians? (See information on <u>Resource Sheet 6A</u>. Also, Jews kept to themselves and prophets often preached only to the Jews. Crossing racial lines may have been distasteful to Jonah.)

2. How do you explain Jonah's ability to sleep even though he was fleeing God and it was storming all around him?

SUMMARY OPTION: *Read Jonah 1:11–17* or summarize it this way: **Jonah confessed that he was at fault and urged them to throw him overboard. After some resistance, they did and he was swallowed by a great fish.**

Read Jonah 2:1–10.

3. What words show that Jonah had a change of heart?

Read Jonah 3:1–4.

4. How did God's instructions to Jonah at the beginning of the book compare with God's instructions to Jonah at the end of the book? (God's instructions didn't change. God didn't ease up when Jonah rebelled. God didn't ease up after restoring Jonah.)

SUMMARY OPTION: *Read Jonah 3:5–10* or summarize it this way: **The Ninevites believed God, repented, and turned from their evil ways. God spared them.**

> **Materials You'll Need For This Session**
>
> Resource Sheet 6A for reference

OPTION
Accountability Partners
Have partners meet and discuss whether they need more understanding that God disciplines the rebellious (justice) or that God restores the rebellious (mercy). Ask them to tell why.

OPTION
Worship Ideas
Read Psalm 120 together as an act of worship.

OPTION
Memory Verse
"From inside the fish Jonah prayed to the Lord his God. He said: 'In my distress I called to the Lord, and he answered me. From the depths of the grave I called for help, and you listened to my cry'"
(Jonah 2:1, 2).

Read Jonah 4:1–10.

5. What reason did Jonah give for being angry?

6. How can you explain that God's compassion would make Jonah angry? (See bottom of <u>Resource Sheet 6A</u> for ideas.)

7. How did God respond to Jonah's anger? (He aroused in Jonah pity for the plant—the same pity that he, the Lord God, had for Nineveh. He also talked with him about it, asking him twice, in verses 4 and 9, the reason for his anger.)

8. In what ways did Jonah rebel?

TAKING THE NEXT STEP

1. Jonah rebelled by hearing a command of God and doing the opposite. What commands of God do we most often rebel against?

2. This passage communicates both justice and mercy: justice because God disciplined Jonah until he obeyed; mercy to restore him even though he rebelled. Consider an area of life in which you are rebelling in some way. (Group members do not need to say out loud what this is.) **Which do you need to be more aware of—God's justice (He will discipline you) or God's mercy (He is willing to restore you)?**

3. OPTION: Have those who believe they need to be more aware of God's justice sit on one side and look up Jonah 2:3, and have those who need to be more aware of God's mercy sit on the other side and find Jonah 2:1, 2. Explain that the group will do a choral response. The *justice* side will go first and read 2:3 together. (Help both sides settle on one Bible version). The mercy side will follow by reading 2:1, 2 together. As the leader, close with 2:9. Go through it twice and then allow a few minutes for reflection at the end.

Jonah at a Glance

✦ *JONAH'S REBELLION*—Read Jonah 1:1–10.

A Difficult Assignment

You may wonder why any prophet who directly hears the voice of God would not do what God asked him to do. We think, "Surely if I heard God's voice, I would go where he wanted me to go!"

Nineveh was not the place you would want to go to preach. You especially would not want to "preach against it" as God commanded. Those people were barbarians. They had been at war with the Israelites and had conquered Jonah's home town. The Ninevites may have even killed Jonah's parents or relatives. And they were famous for their cruel torture of prisoners of war. Stories of Nineveh's torture tactics against Jewish slaves compare with the horrors of Nazi Germany in World War II.

A Rebellious Attitude

You might have expected God to immediately block the way when Jonah ran the other direction. Jonah had no trouble finding a ship ready to leave for Tarshish. He had enough money to pay the fare. He was even able to find a comfortable place below deck to lie down—and he fell asleep! The apparent "open doors" may have allowed him to rationalize it must be the Lord's will for him to do this.

✦ *JONAH'S REPENTANCE*—Read Jonah 2:1–10.

Summary: Jonah confessed that he was at fault and urged them to throw him overboard. After some resistance, they did and he was swallowed by a great fish (1:10–17).

✦ *JONAH'S RESTORATION*—Read Jonah 3:1–4.

Summary: God offered Jonah a second chance, but God didn't change the command.

NINEVEH'S RESPONSE—Jonah 3:5–10
Summary: The Ninevites believed God, repented, and turned from their evil ways. God spared them.

✦ *JONAH'S REGRET*—Read Jonah 4:1–10.

Question: Why was Jonah angry? Perhaps because:
• the Ninevites didn't get what they deserved
• his reputation was tarnished
Summary: God kept asking him questions to help him examine his anger.

—Adapted from *Life Preservers*, by Bob Russell

Finding Restoration

In his book *Life Preservers,* Bob Russell tells this story:

> A friend of mine was an elder in his church when he began a terrible habit of gambling. His habit grew so bad that he began embezzling from his company to pay for his debts. Eventually, to the horror of his family, he was caught and jailed for his behavior.

Point A

> But my friend repented before God and longed to be restored. He humbly and patiently took a servant's role in the church for several years. Then he felt God's call to enter the ministry. He left his job and began working in the church, where today he has a vibrant ministry for Christ.

Point B

♠   ♠   ♠   ♠   ♠   ♠   ♠   ♠   ♠   ♠   ♠

What lies does the enemy feed us to encourage further rebellion?

POINT A (between the first and second paragraphs above):
What lies could have convinced this man not to repent?

POINT B (at the end of the two paragraphs):
What lies could have kept his service from being effective?

Myths About Rebellion

- How does Jonah's story prove or disprove this myth?
- How does the rest of the Scripture prove or disprove this myth?
- What is, in fact, the truth?

MYTH 1: *God doesn't give the rebellious a second chance.*

MYTH 2: *God compromises with the rebellious person—meets him halfway.*

MYTH 3: *Once a person rebels, he's out.*

Seven

God's Promises in Times of Guilt

7 he United States government has had a "conscience fund" for many years to provide relief for people who feel guilty about cheating the government.

- In 1974 someone wrote, "I am sending ten dollars for the blanket I stole while I was in World War II. My mind could not rest. I am sorry I'm late." It was signed, "An ex-GI. PS: I want to be ready to meet God."
- One man sent $150, admitting that he had cheated on his income taxes. His letter concluded, "If I still can't sleep, I'll send the rest later."

We all know what it means to feel guilty. The Bible is full of Scriptures that reveal God's comforting promises for times when we feel guilty.

—Adapted from *Life Preservers,* by Bob Russell

Central Theme	Repentance involves discerning true guilt from false guilt, admitting that guilt, and finding forgiveness in Christ.
Lesson Aim	Group members will look at false ideas about guilt, consider biblical concepts of guilt and forgiveness, and make decisions about their need for confession and forgiveness.
Bible Background	Matthew 3:1–17; 1 John 1:8, 9
For Further Study	Read Chapter 7 of *Life Preservers.*

PLAN ONE Classes

BUILDING COMMUNITY

Display <u>Transparency 7A</u>, "Been Travelin' Lately?" and say something like, **Today it seems as if guilt is considered a bad or unhealthy feeling. Sometimes people use it to manipulate each other. How can guilt be harmful?** (When it's overdone; when it's turned from culpability for a single act to a character trait that is unchangeable—"You always do such and such!"; when we feel guilty for things that aren't sin.)

Ask, **When is guilt good?** (When we have done or said something wrong and feel convicted about it.)

Do most people have a healthy sense of appropriate guilt?

Tell the class that today's session is about John the Baptist's preaching, which probably produced a lot of appropriate guilt within his hearers.

Before class, ask two or three class members to improvise on a skit. Provide the last line of the main character: "Should I pack my bags now? Am I going on a guilt trip?" If your group needs an idea, use this one involving a child, parent, and grandparent. The child misbehaves, the parent begins to correct the child, the grandparent corrects the parent on how to correct the grandchild. In the middle of the correction, the parent can offer the above line.

CONSIDERING SCRIPTURE

Write these symbols on the chalkboard:

✗ repenting, confessing sin
✓ doing what's right
† finding forgiveness
? anything that confuses you

Distribute copies of <u>Resource Sheet 7A</u>, "Marking in the Margins Allowed!" and pens or pencils. Introduce this activity by saying something like, **One of the themes of John the Baptist's preaching was repentance and confession. Look through today's passage and mark these symbols in the margin.** If class members wish to work with partners, urge them to do so.

Cartoon Talkback
5–10 Minutes

Materials You'll Need For This Session

Resource Sheets 7A and 7B, Transparency 7A, pens or pencils, chalk and chalkboard

OPTION
Improvisational Skit
5 Minutes

Marginal Markings
10–15 Minutes

After they're finished, ask for their findings. Here are some ideas:

✗ (repenting, confession)	Matthew 3:2, 6, 8, 11
✓ (doing what's right)	Matthew 3:3 (make straight paths), 8 (produce fruit . . .), 10 (every tree that does not produce . . .); 1 John 1:9
† (finding forgiveness)	1 John 1:9
? (questions)	consider class members' questions

Ask class members, **What is the role of guilt in the relationship with God?** (True and appropriate guilt helps us sense our sin, which is separation from God, and ask for forgiveness and help from God. This mends the relationship with God.)

OPTION
Color Coding Groups
10–15 Minutes

Use the above activity, but divide the class into groups of four or five and give each group four colored pens. Ask them to color code the phrases on Resource Sheet 7A instead of marking in the margins. For example, red=repentance; blue= righteousness (doing what's right); yellow=forgiveness; green= questions about the text.

TAKING THE NEXT STEP

Survey
15 Minutes

Distribute copies of Resource Sheet 7B, "When Guilt Goes Wrong." Write on the chalkboard these categories:
❏ frequently
❏ somewhat frequently
❏ somewhat infrequently
❏ rarely

Read the first section of the resource sheet together. Ask, **How often would you say this statement is true of you: "We feel guilty over things that aren't sin"?** Pick one of the check box categories on the chalkboard. Point to the first check box and ask for a show of hands. Do the same with the other three check boxes. Ask, **What are some of the things we feel guilty about that aren't really sin?** (Feeling guilty if your house isn't spotless or you don't say yes to every request for volunteers at church. Point out that feeling guilty over the wrong things replaces guilt for things we do that are sin.)

Move on to the next section and ask the same question: **How often would you say this statement is true of you: "We don't feel guilty over things that are sin"?** Refer to the check boxes again. Ask, **What are some of the things we should feel guilty for but don't?** (If you need to get them thinking, suggest this one: Lack of kindness and respect to others—especially those our culture tends to ignore.)

Finally, read the third section and ask, **How often would you say this statement is true of you: "We feel so guilty for our sins that we wonder how God can possibly forgive us"?** Refer to the check boxes again.

Say to class members, **Of the three statements on the resource sheet, pick the one that is most disturbing to you, and silently reread what is written below it. Underline the truths there that are important for you to absorb.** Allow them a few minutes to ponder this.

Distribute half sheets of blank paper and pencils and say to class members, **Take a few minutes to write down four or five things you feel guilty about. Feel free to move your chair away from others, if you wish.** After about three minutes, explain, **Look at your list and review Resource Sheet 7B. Are any of the items things you shouldn't feel guilty for—things over which you had no control or that really aren't sin?** (For example, you're parents divorced, your child was injured, you were laid off.) **Cross those out. Consider now the things that you should feel legitimate guilt for. What do you need to do regarding these items? Confess to those involved? Apologize? Make restitution? Write on the sheet anything that comes to you and consider that for a few minutes.**

As they write, pray that class members will have clear thoughts and honest feelings as they do this exercise.

Self-Evaluation
10 Minutes

Groups

BUILDING COMMUNITY

1. Do you agree or disagree with this statement: *Guilt is good.* **Why?**

2. What is the difference between legitimate guilt and false guilt?

3. When has guilt been a positive force in your life?

CONSIDERING SCRIPTURE

Read Matthew 3:1–17.

1. How would you describe John the Baptist's central message?

2. How did people respond to John the Baptist?

3. How did John the Baptist's message to Pharisees and Sadducees compare with his message to the others? (It was similar—repent—but it was more intense.)

4. What response did John the Baptist anticipate from the Pharisees and Sadducees when he asked them to repent? (They would consider themselves righteous because they were sons of Abraham, v. 9.)

5. What is the consequence of not repenting? (Judgment, v. 12; a winnowing fork is a pitchfork used to toss wheat in the air to separate wheat from chaff. Wheat is the useful part while chaff is the useless outer shell. Chaff is burned, but wheat is gathered.)

6. How did Jesus' baptism "fulfill all righteousness" (v. 15)? (In being baptized, Jesus fulfilled God's mission for him and advanced God's work by showing that obedience and humility were important. Jesus' obedient humility contrasted with the Jewish leaders' unrepentant disobedience.)

Materials You'll Need For This Session

Resource Sheet 7B (optional)

OPTION
Accountability Partners

Emphasize the importance of confidentiality between partners and then ask accountability partners to pray about being willing to confess reasons for guilt to their partners or group. (Don't say, "whatever you're comfortable telling your partner." Confession is never comfortable.)

OPTION
Worship Ideas

Read Psalm 51 together as an act of worship.

OPTION
Memory Verse

"If we claim to be without sin, we deceive ourselves and the truth is not in us. If we confess our sins, he is faithful and just and will forgive us our sins and purify us from all unrighteousness" (1 John 1:8, 9).

Read 1 John 1:8, 9.

7. What is God's response to our confession of sin?

TAKING THE NEXT STEP

Read this situation:

As treasurer of the single adults group at church, Calvin brings home the group's money every weekend to deposit the next Monday. One Monday, he was surprised that some of it was missing. As the week progressed, Calvin remembered how his ten-year-old son, who had visited him the previous weekend, had watched Calvin put the money away. Calvin felt guilty. What was he doing wrong to be raising a son that would take money from a church offering?

How could he have been so careless with the money?

1. How might Calvin feel guilty for something that is not his sin? What should Calvin feel guilty for and correct? How might he feel so guilty that he would assume that he could never be useful in God's service? (Calvin doesn't need to feel guilty for his son's behavior, but he should feel guilty if he doesn't talk with his son, offering consequences and discerning why his son stole the money. Calvin might also examine his methods for handling money and seek more careful methods. If you wish, distribute copies of Resource Sheet 7B for further discussion of the above questions.)

2. OPTION: What do the verses we studied tell us about handling guilt over past sins? (The first passage commands people to repent, which involves true and healthy guilt. The 1 John passage tells how to find forgiveness, and as a result, relief from guilt.)

3. OPTION: How has false guilt (feeling guilty over things that aren't sin or aren't our responsibility) tripped you up in the past? (It often distracts us from the things we should feel guilty about and misleads our conscience into thinking true repentance has occurred.)

4. In what areas of your life do you need a sense of repentance—true guilt?

Marking in the Margins Allowed!

This isn't a library book or a borrowed book—it's your copy of Scripture and you can mark in the margins, even draw in them if you want!

Matthew 3	Margin

Matthew 3

1 In those days John the Baptist came, preaching in the Desert of Judea 2 and saying, "Repent, for the kingdom of heaven is near." 3 This is he who was spoken of through the prophet Isaiah: "A voice of one calling in the desert, 'Prepare the way for the Lord, make straight paths for him.'" 4 John's clothes were made of camel's hair, and he had a leather belt around his waist. His food was locusts and wild honey. 5 People went out to him from Jerusalem and all Judea and the whole region of the Jordan. 6 Confessing their sins, they were baptized by him in the Jordan River. 7 But when he saw many of the Pharisees and Sadducees coming to where he was baptizing, he said to them: "You brood of vipers! Who warned you to flee from the coming wrath? 8 Produce fruit in keeping with repentance. 9 And do not think you can say to yourselves, 'We have Abraham as our father.' I tell you that out of these stones God can raise up children for Abraham. 10 The ax is already at the root of the trees, and every tree that does not produce good fruit will be cut down and thrown into the fire. 11 I baptize you with water for repentance. But after me will come one who is more powerful than I, whose sandals I am not fit to carry. He will baptize you with the Holy Spirit and with fire. 12 His winnowing fork is in his hand, and he will clear his threshing floor, gathering his wheat into the barn and burning up the chaff with unquenchable fire." 13 Then Jesus came from Galilee to the Jordan to be baptized by John. 14 But John tried to deter him, saying, "I need to be baptized by you, and do you come to me?" 15 Jesus replied, "Let it be so now; it is proper for us to do this to fulfill all righteousness." Then John consented. 16 As soon as Jesus was baptized, he went up out of the water. At that moment heaven was opened, and he saw the Spirit of God descending like a dove and lighting on him. 17 And a voice from heaven said, "This is my Son, whom I love; with him I am well pleased."

1 John 1:8, 9

8 If we claim to be without sin, we deceive ourselves and the truth is not in us. 9 If we confess our sins, he is faithful and just and will forgive us our sins and purify us from all unrighteousness.

When Guilt Goes Wrong

WE FEEL GUILTY OVER THINGS THAT AREN'T SIN.

People feel guilty about things that are not sins. One mother might feel guilty if her house is not spotless. A young couple might feel guilty if they have nicer things than most couples. Some adult children are made to feel guilty by their parents for not visiting as often as they would like. You may feel guilty if you do not say yes to every request for volunteers at church. I used to feel guilty if I wasn't working all the time. I even felt guilty if I got a telephone call at 3 A.M. and I was asleep! I'd clear my throat and say, "Hello," like I had been up praying, just waiting for the telephone call.

WE DON'T FEEL GUILTY OVER THINGS THAT ARE SIN.

Our conscience is like a computer. It spits out whatever had been programmed into it. If we feed it the wrong information, it will alarm us at the wrong times. That is why it is important to continue to study the Word of God, which never changes. God's standards of morality are eternal and are not open for negotiation. His laws remain even if the whole world rejects them.

WE FEEL SO GUILTY FOR OUR SINS THAT WE WONDER HOW GOD CAN POSSIBLY FORGIVE US.

It is sometimes difficult to believe God could really forgive our sins. "You don't know what I've done," someone will say. "There is no way God could forgive me." But to make that claim is to show a lack of faith in the promise of God. He knows what you did. He knew what you were going to do when he made those promises. He paid for your sin on the cross. The Bible tells us what God does with sin:

- God removes our sins as far as the east is from the west (Psalm 103:11, 12).
- God forgets (Isaiah 43:14, 25).
- Our sins disappear like morning dew (Isaiah 44:6, 22).
- God buries our sins in the depths of the sea (Micah 7:18, 19).
- Though our sins are scarlet, God makes them white as snow (Isaiah 1:18).

Because of the sacrifice of Christ, you have a permanent "not guilty" stamp on you. Your sins have already been paid for.

—Adapted from *Life Preservers,* by Bob Russell

Been Travelin' Lately?

"Uh oh, are you telling me to pack my bags—
'cause I'm goin' on a guilt trip?"

Eight

God's Promises in Times of Worry

Worry and anxiety sap our energy, divert our attention, and waste our time. One study on the subject of worry revealed what we worry about:

- Forty percent of our worries never happen.
- Thirty percent are concerns of the past that we cannot change anyway.
- Twelve percent are needless worries about our health.
- Eight percent are legitimate concerns.

Worry is considered a "respectable" sin. If someone worries, he will be more likely to admit that sin publicly than the sins of the flesh such as adultery, shoplifting, or murder. Yet Jesus condemned worry as a sign of little faith.

Anxiety is hard on your body. Fifty percent of the people with anxiety disorders have seen a physician in the past six months for physical symptoms relating to anxiety. They consult neurologists for dizziness, gastroenterologists for digestive disorders, cardiologists for chest pains, and respiratory specialists for shortness of breath.

Jesus was right. It doesn't pay to worry.

—Adapted from *Life Preservers*, by Bob Russell

Central Theme	When we offer God our worries, he can replace them with an incomprehensible peace.
Lesson Aim	Group members will look at ways in which they worry and consider how to trust God with worries.
Bible Background	Mark 4:35–41; Matthew 6:25, 34
For Further Study	Read Chapter 8 of *Life Preservers*.

Classes

BUILDING COMMUNITY

Display <u>Transparency 8A</u>, "Worry Styles." Ask class members, **Which style would your friend/spouse/child say you are?** You may want to start out, "I used to be . . . but now I lean toward . . ." to get class members talking.

Tell the class members that **This session is about worry and how God stands with us in worry even when it looks as if he isn't doing anything to resolve the problem that worries us, which is how the disciples felt in today's passage.**

Write this sentence on the chalkboard, "I never worry. I just_____." Explain, **We tend to think of worriers as people who wring their hands endlessly, wailing and complaining. Worrying is an individual thing. For example, some might complete this sentence, "I don't worry, I hold it all in. I don't worry, I pretend nothing bothers me. I don't worry, I only slightly brood over things." What do you do—instead of worrying?** Try to keep this discussion light—using a humorous example, if you can—so that class members will feel free to reveal their ways of worrying.

CONSIDERING SCRIPTURE

Ask someone to read **Mark 4:35–41** aloud, and have the class divide into groups. Distribute paper and pencils to each group and appoint a recorder for each group. Explain, **Retell this biblical account, but put it in today's times. First, choose a disaster—something life-threatening, but not uncommon. Then decide: What would the disciples say to show their anxiety? How would Jesus stand by them and miraculously dispel their fear?** The groups do not have to write out their story, but they'll probably want to make a few notes.

After a few minutes, the groups should be in the middle of writing their stories. Ask them to pause, and distribute copies of <u>Resource Sheet 8A</u>, "God's Promises to Those Who Worry." Ask volunteers to read it. Then ask the group, **In light of the thoughts expressed on this sheet, look at your story again. Try to incorporate these ideas into Jesus' speech and behavior in your story.**

Choosing Categories
5 Minutes

Sentence Completion
5–8 Minutes

Materials You'll Need For This Session

Resource Sheets 8A and 8B, Transparency 8A, pens or pencils, chalk and chalkboard

Parallel Story
10–15 Minutes

Give the groups a few more minutes, and then ask a volunteer from each group to tell the story. Note when the groups incorporate ideas from Resource Sheet 8A: Christ as a compassionate friend; Christ providing daily what is needed; Christ giving unexplainable peace.

Monologues
10–15 Minutes

Ask a volunteer to read aloud *Mark 4:35–41*. If you did not pass out copies of Transparency 8A, do so now. Divide the class into four groups and ask all members of each group to imagine that they are one of Jesus' disciples who was on the boat. Assign one of the four personalities on the transparency to each group and have each group answer these two questions.

- **Based on your assigned personality, what did you (the disciple) think during the storm? While Jesus seemed unaware and unconcerned—fast asleep—what were you thinking?**
- **After Jesus calmed the storm, what did you think? How did you feel?**

As the four groups work, urge them to choose a volunteer to present their imaginary disciples' thoughts and feelings.

After a few minutes, read Mark 4:35–41 again. Ask a volunteer from each group either to share the ideas of the group or to present that imaginary disciple's responses, beginning with, "I felt . . ."

TAKING THE NEXT STEP

Personalizing Scripture
5 Minutes

Direct class members' attention once again to Resource Sheet 8A. Explain, **Choose one of the Scriptures on the page and underline it. Then, at the bottom of the sheet or on the opposite side, paraphrase that verse in such a way that the verse becomes a personal message from God to you. For example, John 14:1 can be personalized, "I won't let my heart be troubled. I trust in God."** If you have time, ask class members to read the personalized verses to the entire class.

OPTION
Breath Prayers
5 Minutes

Distribute copies of Resource Sheet 8B, "Create Your Own 'Breath Prayer.'" Read together the questions at the top and the first step. Give participants a minute to do the first step and then read the second one. Read Step 2 instructions and give them a few minutes. Read Step 3 instructions and give them a few minutes. Ask any class member who wishes to share his or her breath prayer to do so. If members find another person's prayer has more meaning for them, urge them to write it down as well. Finally, read the instructions for Step 4 and pray for class members as they list the times of day when a breath prayer would be useful.

Groups

BUILDING COMMUNITY

Distribute magazines. (News, parenting, and general interest magazines work well.) Allow group members to work with partners if they wish.

1. Look through one of the magazines and tear out an advertisement or article that represents something people worry about.

2. Why do people worry? (If you wish, read from Resource Sheet 8A, especially the fourth paragraph under "Provisions One Day at a Time," which begins, "It is challenging . . .")

3. What are some of the less obvious ways that people behave when they worry? What are some less obvious symptoms of worry?

CONSIDERING SCRIPTURE

Read Mark 4:35–41.

1. What seemed to upset the disciples most, based on their complaint to Jesus? (They assumed that because he was asleep, Jesus was unaware and unconcerned.)

2. What did the disciples come away knowing that they didn't know before? (That Jesus was aware and concerned; that he was powerful enough to control the wind and sea—maybe he was the Christ!)

3. In what respect did the disciples have "no faith" (v. 40)? (The disciples had seen Jesus heal several people miraculously, so they should have suspected that he could intervene in the storm. Yet it's easier to believe in God's power to heal someone else's circumstances than one's own. Or, perhaps they did suspect he could intervene, but they became annoyed that he didn't wake up. This too would be a lack of faith that Jesus would help them.)

Materials You'll Need For This Session

Enough magazines so that there's at least one for every two group members, Resource Sheet 8A and 8B (optional)

OPTION
Accountability Partners
Have partners meet and discuss specific worries that they need to turn over to God. Encourage them to pray for each other.

OPTION
Worship Ideas
Read Psalm 40 together as an act of worship.

OPTION
Memory Verse
"Therefore do not worry about tomorrow, for tomorrow will worry about itself. Each day has enough trouble of its own" (Matthew 6:34).

Read Matthew 6:25–34.

4. Why do people who obviously have enough food and clothing still fuss and worry about these things?

5. What has medical research discovered that proves verse 27? (Worry doesn't add to your life; it takes away health and longevity. If you wish, read the third paragraph from the introduction, beginning with the sentence, "Anxiety is hard on your body . . .")

6. What do you think it means to "seek first his kingdom" (v. 33)? (To make our first concern our relationship with God and the doing of his will through communicating the truth about who Jesus Christ is and showing mercy and justice.)

7. Consider verse 34. What is the difference between planning for tomorrow and worrying about it? (Planning involves setting goals, procedures, and schedules. When those plans are riddled with fear, worry abounds.)

TAKING THE NEXT STEP

1. Complete this sentence: Turning worries over to God means . . .

2. What can we do when we find ourselves worrying after turning over worries to God? (Turn them over again. Each time is another opportunity to pray and God enjoys our prayers and wants us to depend on him continually. Use Resource Sheet 8B, if you wish, to help group members create a breath prayer.)

3. What principle from today's passages would be most helpful to you to remember as you turn over worries to God?

God's Promises to Those Who Worry

THE PRESENCE OF A COMPASSIONATE FRIEND

God is always with us. He has given us the Holy Spirit—a constant companion, counselor, comforter, and friend. We should not worry about facing the world alone or making wrong decisions or "doing something stupid," because God has promised us the great Counselor to guide and comfort us.

> *"Do not let your hearts be troubled. Trust in God; trust also in me. . . . And I will ask the Father, and he will give you another Counselor to be with you forever . . . But the Counselor, the Holy Spirit, whom the Father will send in my name, will teach you all things and will remind you of everything I have said to you" (John 14:1, 16, 26).*

PROVISIONS ONE DAY AT A TIME

> *"Therefore I tell you, do not worry about your life, what you will eat or drink; or about your body, what you will wear. Is not life more important than food, and the body more important than clothes? . . . Therefore do not worry about tomorrow, for tomorrow will worry about itself. Each day has enough trouble of its own" (Matthew 6:25, 34).*

These words were spoken nearly 2,000 years ago, but Jesus knew what we needed to hear. We chase after the same things the pagans chase after, and we teach our children to do the same. We worry about what we will eat: Will everyone like the dinner? Can we find a place to eat out that everyone likes? Will there be enough money to eat on before the next paycheck?

We worry about what we will wear: Is this dress in style? Do my shirts have the right labels on them? Is my tie too wide or too narrow? Will the holes in my socks show?

It is challenging to depend completely on God to provide instead of our own efforts. We do not like giving up control, and that is why we worry. Somehow we think if we worry enough we will be on guard, we will be prepared, we won't be surprised, we might even have a chance to change the outcome of some terrible experience. That is a lie from Satan.

You may decide to give up control of a part of your life, then discover later you have tried to wrestle control back from God. Trusting in God's daily provisions for our needs is a constant discipline.

PEACE THAT PASSES UNDERSTANDING

> *"Do not be anxious about anything, but in everything, by prayer and petition, with thanksgiving, present your requests to God. And the peace of God, which transcends all understanding, will guard your hearts and your minds in Christ Jesus" (Philippians 4:6, 7).*

First, Paul says, make a choice that you are not going to worry. Second, pray about everything. Tell God about it. Do not try to control it on your own. Third, pray with thanksgiving. Nothing changes your attitude like gratitude. If you have trouble falling asleep because you are worried, tell God the things you are thankful for. Go through the alphabet. Start with "A" and think of all the things you are thankful for that start with that letter, no matter how big or small. You probably won't get to "Z" without falling asleep.

—Adapted from *Life Preservers,* by Bob Russell

Create Your Own "Breath Prayer"

What is a "breath prayer"?
A familiar prayer of nine or ten syllables or less that has great meaning for me.

Why?
The process of turning worries over to God repeatedly doesn't seem so irksome.

Step 1: Pick a phrase from Scripture or Resource Sheet 8A that describes what you need from God when you turn worries over to him.

>Examples:
>You are present with me.
>Give me peace that passes all understanding.
>Take away my troubles.

Your choice: _____

Step 2: Pick a favorite name for God.

>Examples:
>Compassionate Friend
>Father in Heaven
>Creator-God

Your choice: _____

Step 3: Combine the two above parts in a way that rolls off your tongue.

>Examples:
>You are present, my Compassionate Friend.
>Take my worries, Father in Heaven.

Your choice: _____

Step 4: Practice it when you're worried this week and don't be embarrassed at having to repeat it over and over. That's what it's for!

List a few times in an average day when it would be helpful to use this breath prayer.

_____   _____

_____   _____

Worry Styles

BOB the BROODER

My boss said the weirdest thing and
I can't quit thinking about it.

If I just hadn't quit that job I had ten
years ago, I'd be better off today.

ILEANA the INTERNALIZER

I don't worry, but I get headaches.

Every time I start a new job,
I break out in a rash.

PAUL the PESSIMIST

Sooner or later, I'm going
to have a heart attack.

I knew this sink
would leak someday.

SALLY the SCREAMER

I'm worried that my husband
is two hours late from work,
so I yell at my kids.

I worry that my son may be
taking drugs, so I yell at him.

Nine

God's Promises
in Times of Opposition

Robert Hussein, a Kuwaiti convert to Christianity, went on trial for apostasy—abandonment of Islam. According to the Washington *Times*, if convicted, he faces the forced dissolution of his marriage and the loss of certain civil rights, including the right to see his children. He fears that some Muslims would interpret a guilty ruling as permission to kill him, because there is no punishment for killing an apostate of Islam.

The example of other Christians should encourage us when we face opposition: the threat of divorce; pressure to give in or lose your job; betrayal by a close friend. In the face of opposition such as the early Christians in today's passage faced, I'd be tempted to gripe, grow bitter, give in, and promise never to preach in that city again, but the leaders of the early church didn't do those things.

—Adapted from *Life Preservers*, by Bob Russell

Central Theme   Christians can get beyond opposition and criticism by keeping their focus on God, pleasing Christ instead of pleasing others.

Lesson Aim   Group members will discover biblical principles for facing opposition and criticism and evaluate ways that work best for them.

Bible Background   Acts 16:11–40

For Further Study   Read Chapter 9 of *Life Preservers*.

PLAN ONE

Classes

BUILDING COMMUNITY

▢ Display Transparency 9A, "Dear Abby Revisited," and read the top portion together. (Just for fun, jiggle the transparency a little as Kurt does in the story.) As you read the second part, "The Plot Thickens . . ." feel free to cross out the italicized roles and insert a role that people in your community revere (for example, mayor, PTA president, or union president).

After class members have offered their reactions, summarize by saying that we respond to opposition in a variety of ways, and today's lesson will look at this issue.

▢ Have the class form groups of three and ask someone to volunteer from each group. Explain, **I will tell the volunteer from your group a certain word. When I give the signal, this person will act out the word but say nothing and make no noise. When your group guesses the word correctly, your entire group may stand up.**

Call the volunteers up front and tell them that the word is *criticism,* and remind them to wait for the signal to begin. After they have returned to their groups and everyone is seated, give the signal to begin.

CONSIDERING SCRIPTURE

▢ Distribute copies of Resource Sheet 9A, "Key Events in Acts 16:11–40." Ask a volunteer to read the first section on the sheet, *Acts 16:11–15,* and then say, **Look at the first section on the sheet. Place a check by whether this passage presents Paul's work as a success—meaning times in which God's kingdom is advanced—or whether he faced criticism and opposition.**

Ask another volunteer to read *Acts 16:16–18,* and ask for the class's responses on the sheet. Do the same with *Acts 16:19–24* and then *16:25–34.*

Ask another volunteer to read *Acts 16:35–40,* and ask for members' responses to the question on the sheet. Also ask, **In what ways did Paul and Silas respond to opposition and criticism well?** (In this passage, they didn't respond until they were let go. Then Paul protested his treatment and demanded to be

Dear Abby Revisited
7 Minutes

OPTION
Word Pantomime
5 Minutes

▢ **Materials You'll Need For This Session**

Resource Sheets 9A and 9B, Transparency 9A, pens or pencils, chalk and chalkboard

Categorizing Events
20 Minutes

escorted. Another "response," of sorts, was their calmness and hymn singing in prison [v. 25].)

When you're finished, ask, if you wish, **What principles about facing opposition can we glean from Paul's behavior?** (Paul confronted the troubled person [v. 18], prayed and sang hymns [v. 25], defended his rights [v. 37], and encouraged others [v. 40].)

OPTION
Inventing Subtitles
10–15 Minutes

Read the following portions of *Acts 16* in these sections:
16:11–15
16:16–18
16:19–24
16:25–34
16:35–40

After having a volunteer read the first section, ask class members to think of a short subtitle for that section. For example, the subtitle for this first section could be "Early Success in Philippi." Do the same with the other passages, writing each subtitle on the chalkboard.

OPTION
Cartoon Strip
15 Minutes

Have the class form groups of three or four members, and assign each group one of the five passages listed above. Give each group a sheet of paper and pencils, and ask students to condense their section into one frame of a cartoon strip. Encourage them to use stick figures; time doesn't permit anything more.

When everyone is finished, tape the scenes to the wall in the proper order and view them as a class. If your class is large, this might work better on transparencies, so you can display them on the overhead projector.

TAKING THE NEXT STEP

Brainstorming
10 Minutes

Read together Resource Sheet 9B, "Handling Criticism." Then ask the class to help you list on the chalkboard ten specific things Christians can do to stay focused on God in the midst of opposition, especially criticism. Urge them to suggest things they've never tried, but they think might work. You might ask these questions if they are stumped:
- **What helps you ignore the criticism if it's wrong?** (Stay busy with the task at hand.)
- **What helps you evaluate the criticism?** (Pray, talk with someone you respect.)
- **What does God say to do in response to enemies?** (Pray for them, love them—do something nice for the person who criticizes you.)

Close by having each person pick one of the ways listed he or she needs to consider using next time he or she faces opposition.

Read together <u>Resource Sheet 9B</u>, "Handling Criticism." Explain, **Think of something you can do to stay focused on God—and in doing so, avoid being discouraged by opposition. Once you've thought of a way to do this, don't say it out loud. Raise your hand when you've gotten this far.** Wait a few minutes. **Now, stand up and pose in a way that illustrates your idea. Don't move—behave like a stone sculpture. For example, if your idea is to read the Bible, especially Psalms, for encouragement, stand up, turn to Psalms and stand in a reading pose. If you have an idea, but can't think of how to turn it into a "sculpture," whisper it to someone else and let them try it.**

After each person with an idea offers it (don't be discouraged if some don't want to do this in front of the class), ask that person some questions, if appropriate: **How does that help you stay focused on God? What made you think of this? Have you tried this? If so, how has it worked for you?**

Encourage each class member to consider a new way to stay focused on God that was presented in this lesson.

PLAN TWO

Groups

BUILDING COMMUNITY

1. **Tell about a time when you saw someone criticized and that person behaved in a way that seemed wise. Perhaps he ignored the criticism or responded quietly, or defended himself in an unusually composed manner.** (Be ready with an example of your own, if possible.)

2. **How do you usually respond to opposition?**
   ❏ **I'm open to hearing what's said.**
   ❏ **I tune it out.**
   ❏ **I like to get even.**

3. **Jesus said to pray for those who persecute you (Matthew 5:44). What prayer can we possibly offer for people who oppose us?**

CONSIDERING SCRIPTURE

Read Acts 16:11–15.

1. **What does this passage show about Paul's initiative and leadership?** (He went to leading cities, found places of prayer, and put himself forward to speak.)

2. **How does the text describe the process Lydia went through when hearing Paul?** (v. 14)

Read Acts 16:16–24.

3. **How does Lydia, the hostess of Paul and his friends, compare with the woman described next?** (The Philippian church must have been full of contrasts—rich people like Lydia and a slave girl, among others.)

4. **What persecution did Paul and Silas suffer?**

Read Acts 16:25–40.

Accountability Partners
Have partners discuss who they feel opposed by and how they would like to behave the next time that person opposes them. Urge them to take time to pray for that person who opposes them.

OPTION
Worship Ideas
Read Psalm 27 together as an act of worship.

OPTION
Memory Verse
"About midnight Paul and Silas were praying and singing hymns to God, and the other prisoners were listening to them" (Acts 16:25).

5. How do the actions of Paul and Silas in prison show they were focused on God and not preoccupied with their persecution? (They prayed and sang, and when the right opportunity arose, they evangelized instead of escaping!)

6. How would you describe the radical change in the jailer's attitude toward his prisoners while they were there?

7. Why do you think Paul defended Silas and himself at the end when they didn't defend themselves earlier? (It's difficult to know. Perhaps they wanted to speak up to protect other believers from getting the same treatment.)

8. What does Paul and Silas's behavior tell us about responding to opposition? (If you wish, distribute copies of Resource Sheet 9B, "Handling Criticism," and ask which of the items listed apply to Paul's situation, either as stated in the text or obvious from implication.)

TAKING THE NEXT STEP

Have group members think of a time when they felt opposed by someone—at work, at home, in the neighborhood, in the church. Ask them not to mention that person's name, but answer these questions.

1. Was Person X opposing you maliciously or do you think that person honestly thought you were wrong or doing someone harm?

2. What is it you would like for Person X to do or to say?

3. Were you able to stay focused on God in the midst of Person X's opposition? If so, how?

4. What would you like to be able to do next time Person X (or a similar person) opposes you?

Key Events in Acts 16:11-40

Acts 16:11–15

Check one: Paul and his group . . .

_____ were a success (meaning God's kingdom was advanced)

_____ faced opposition and criticism

Acts 16:16–18

Check one: Paul and Silas . . .

_____ were a success (meaning God's kingdom was advanced)

_____ faced opposition and criticism

Acts 16:19–24

Check one: Paul and Silas . . .

_____ were a success (meaning God's kingdom was advanced)

_____ faced opposition and criticism

Acts 16:25–34

Check one: Paul and Silas . . .

_____ were a success (meaning God's kingdom was advanced)

_____ faced opposition and criticism

Acts 16:35–40

Check one: Paul and Silas . . .

_____ were a success (meaning God's kingdom was advanced)

_____ faced opposition and criticism

Handling Criticism

*D*EALING WITH CRITICISM and confrontation is probably the closest most of us get to dealing with true persecution.

1. Expect to be criticized, especially if you're a leader.

If you carry the ball, you are going to get tackled. Negative notes and phone calls, petty comments and anonymous letters are inevitable. Jesus said, "No servant is greater than his master. If they persecuted me, they will persecute you also" (John 15:20).

2. Evaluate the source.

Is it a petty, small-minded person who is griping, or someone whom you respect? If criticism comes from a constant complainer, ignore it and go on.

3. Weigh the objection.

The objection might be valid. If so, then thank the person for his concern and make the necessary adjustment. If it is based on untruth, ignore it. Truth has a way of surfacing in time. When you answer an untrue criticism, you usually give it more validity than it merits.

4. Keep your focus.

Do not grumble about the critics. Do not let Satan distract you from your primary purpose. Your assignment is to please Christ, not men. His is the only opinion that really matters. People are fickle. The same people who criticize you today may be singing your praises tomorrow. "Make up your mind not to worry beforehand how you will defend yourselves. For I will give you words and wisdom that none of your adversaries will be able to resist or contradict" (Luke 21:14, 15).

5. Maintain a sense of humor.

Sometimes you have to maintain a sense of humor about the opposition you face. A skeptical reporter once saw Billy Graham disembark the Queen Mary and quipped, "When Jesus was on the earth, he rode a lowly donkey. I can't imagine Jesus arriving from England on a luxury ocean liner."

Grady Wilson, one of Graham's associates, responded, "Find me a donkey that can swim the Atlantic and I'll buy it!"

6. Give God thanks.

Jesus said, "Blessed are you when people insult you . . . because of me" (Matthew 5:11). When you can receive criticism with thanks and praise to God, then you will know you are growing in faith and love.

—Adapted from *Life Preservers,* by Bob Russell

Dear Abby
Revisited

IMAGINE . . .

Kurt is in charge of changing transparencies for the overhead projector, either for the song service at church or during the pastor's sermon. Kurt hasn't put up any transparencies upside down yet, but he has jiggled a few transparencies now and then. Once he cut off the bottom by not showing it.

Kurt has received criticism about these things, as well as these:

- *Overhead projectors are a tool of the devil.*

- *In my day, we didn't use those things.*

- *Black and white looks dowdy—where's the color?*

THE PLOT THICKENS . . .

Let's say Kurt writes to a Dear Abby character and asks for advice.

- If she's a *peaceful grandmother type*, what do you think she would say?

- If she's a *former biker*, what do you think she would say?

- If she's a *social worker*, what do you think she would say?

Ten

God's Promises in Times of Prosperity

More people are ruined during prosperous times than during times of adversity. The Bible is full of examples of people who began with a close walk with God, but drifted away when they became successful in the eyes of the world. King Saul was so self-conscious when he was first anointed king that he hid from the crowd. But after a few years of success, he became so arrogant that he attempted to kill his successor.

David was so pure when he was a boy that he was described as a man after God's own heart. But after his success as king, he committed adultery and murder and became a passive, overindulgent father.

Solomon began his political career by humbly asking for wisdom. God prospered him beyond measure, but in time Solomon played the fool and married 700 wives.

—Adapted from *Life Preservers,* by Bob Russell

Central Theme	While prosperity often makes people self-absorbed, God can help us to use prosperity to do his will in the world and bless others.
Lesson Aim	Group members will look at how easy it is to go astray when prosperous, and will consider attitudes and behaviors that can help them avoid this.
Bible Background	Genesis 41:46–57; 45:1–11; 50:15–23
For Further Study	Read Chapter 10 of *Life Preservers*.

Classes

BUILDING COMMUNITY

Write this heading on the chalkboard: "10 Bad Habits of Highly Successful People." Below the heading, write the numbers 1–10 in a column on the left. Ask class members, **Help me make a list of negative attitudes and behaviors that people tend to slip into once they become successful.** If your class members get stuck, ask questions, such as, **What about finances? What about family? What about job performance or work ethic?** Explain that today's session is about how to maintain integrity and closeness to God even when you prosper.

Read the quote from Bob Russell in the introduction (p. 109). Then say, **If each of these men could describe their lives, they might say, "I was doing fine until things improved! Then . . ." Can you think of times in your own life or someone else's life when that was true—you were close to God, or you had your spending under control—but then things got better?** You might give them an example from your life to get them started. As each class member responds, thank him or her for contributing to the discussion.

CONSIDERING SCRIPTURE

Display <u>Transparency 10A</u>, and explain, **Even though Joseph became prosperous, he managed to keep his godly perspective.** Read the items in the left column of the transparency and assign the following texts to different volunteers to be read aloud: *Genesis 41:46–57; 45:1–11; 50:15–23.* (If you wish, write their names next to the assigned Scripture on the transparency in the lower left column.) Before they read, say, **As these passages are read, listen for the characteristics listed here on the transparency. You may want to follow along in your own Bible so you can note the verse references.**

When the passage has been read, ask class members to tell which verses show Joseph behaving in the following ways and write them in the right column of the transparency:

Diligent on the job for a prolonged period: 41:56; 45:6. (Joseph was still working hard after seven years of abundance and two more years of famine.)

Brainstorming
5 Minutes

Sentence Completion
10 Minutes

Materials You'll Need For This Session

Resource Sheets 10A and 10B, Transparency 10A, pens or pencils, chalk and chalkboard

---

Verse Find
10–15 Minutes

Remained faithful to his wife and grateful for his children: 41:50–52; 50:22, 23. (This is proven even more by what isn't recorded—no unfaithfulness, no marrying more than one wife.)

Used his position to benefit others: 45:10, 11; 50:19–21. (Joseph also benefited the entire nation of Egypt and surrounding nations. He could have been bitter toward Egypt, which had been his land of captivity, but he was generous.)

Understood God as the source of his prosperity: 45:7, 8. (He never considered himself a self-made man.)

OPTION
Filling in the Gaps
5 Minutes

For those who are unfamiliar with the story of Joseph or may not recall the details, refer to the lower portion of Transparency 10A, "What Joseph Did Right." Before reading each passage listed on the left, have someone read the background listed to the right of it.

OPTION
Path of Life Diagram
15 Minutes

Draw a vertical line from the bottom of the chalkboard to the top, and explain, **This represents Joseph's life. He managed to do a lot of things right even though he was prosperous.**

Draw three or more lines shooting off to the sides from this basic line. Explain, **These are ways Joseph could have gone wrong in his days of prosperity.** Then give the background (see bottom of Transparency 10A), and have a volunteer read the first passage, *Genesis 41:41–57*. Say, **We see how Joseph did behave. How could he have gone wrong in his success?** (He could have become proud and greedy, embezzling during the plentiful years. He could have taken many wives.) Write each of their suggestions on a different offshoot from the original line.

Then have someone read *Genesis 45:1–11*, and do the same. (He could have done the same as above, or refused to forgive his brothers.)

Repeat the process with *Genesis 50:15–23*. (He could have inflicted revenge on his brothers or become self-indulgent and complacent.)

TAKING THE NEXT STEP

Paraphrase and Discussion
10–15 Minutes

Distribute copies of Resource Sheet 10A, "Good News, Bad News of Prosperity," and have several people take turns reading portions of it. Explain, **You may wonder how you could be considered prosperous. Most of our class members are, however, prosperous by global standards. Only a small percentage of the world's population owns a car. Two-thirds of the people of the world eat mostly rice and beans, but most of us have more choices. Globally speaking, most of us are very prosperous.**

(Pray for wisdom in presenting this and choose words carefully. You may have some class members who are extremely well off, and this will take the spotlight off them. And, there may be other class members struggling financially—bankruptcy is not uncommon—but they haven't told anyone in the class.)

Have another class member read the memory verse at the bottom of Resource Sheet 10A. Distribute pens or pencils, and say to class members, **Paraphrase this verse for yourself—either below the verse or on the other side of the paper. Keep in mind Joseph's understanding that God used Joseph's prosperity for God's causes, including the cause of blessing other people.**

Then ask class members, **How is this verse true for you and your situation? Has anything that looked devastating turned out to be for God's purposes?**

Distribute copies of Resource Sheet 10B, "Using Prosperity for God's Purposes." Explain, **Based on the things that Joseph did right (listed at the top), here are some ideas to consider. Fill this out, but you don't need to show it to anyone.** After they've finished, urge them to ask God to show them where they need to let him change them.

OPTION
Self-Evaluation
5 Minutes

*G*roups

BUILDING COMMUNITY

1. Has it been easier for you to be faithful in times of adversity or times of ease?

OPTION: Distribute copies of <u>Resource Sheet 10A</u>, "Good News, Bad News of Prosperity," and ask several volunteers to read the added temptations of the prosperous at the top.

2. Of the temptations listed at the top, what has been most difficult for you in times of ease?

OPTION: Read the introduction at the beginning of the lesson.

3. All of these men loved God, but they had trouble handling success. Why does that happen?

CONSIDERING SCRIPTURE

If you wish, read background materials from the bottom of <u>Transparency 10A</u> before each passage.

Read Genesis 41:46–57.

1. Besides being the "idea man" for storing the grain, what else did Joseph do?

2. What do the names that Joseph gave his sons reveal about his attitude toward them?

3. What does Pharaoh's behavior toward Joseph tell you about Joseph's trustworthiness through all those years of abundance (and great possibilities for embezzlement)?

Read Genesis 45:1–11.

4. What did Joseph say about how God worked out his purposes in Joseph's life?

> **Materials You'll Need For This Session**
>
> Resource Sheets 10A and 10B, Transparency 10A (optional)

5. How did Joseph show his concern for his family—even though his brothers betrayed him?

Read Genesis 50:15–23.

6. What does this passage tell you about the character of Joseph?

7. How did Joseph use his position to benefit others?

8. From what you've read about Joseph in these passages, what do you know about his:
- **Ability to stay diligent on the job for a prolonged period?**
- **Marriage and relationship with his children?** (They appear to have stayed in tact.)

9. How did Joseph manage to be a success personally and spiritually in ways that other Old Testament heroes did not? (If you haven't yet read the introduction to this session, do so now.)

TAKING THE NEXT STEP

1. Pretend you are writing a letter of advice to a young adult—about 25 years old—who is happily married and has a good job. Based on what you have seen that Joseph did right, what would you tell that person? (Distribute copies of Resource Sheet 10A if you haven't already done so.)

OPTION: If you wish, distribute copies of Resource Sheet 10B, "Using Prosperity for God's Purposes," and ask group members to read the entire sheet.

2. Of the four areas listed at the top, which is most difficult for you?

Good News, Bad News of Prosperity

Bad News: Added Temptations of the Prosperous

PRIDE: Gordon MacDonald has said that few things kill the soul faster than becoming addicted to the applause of people. Such acclaim has a narcotic effect on our perception of the reality of our sinful predicament and our daily dependence on the operating grace of God.

INDULGENCE: One study revealed that in 1950 Americans spent 10 percent of their income on luxuries. By 1980 we were spending 30 percent on luxuries. Albert Schweitzer, the famous missionary, almost always wore the same suit. He had one that he had worn for 40 years, and one black tie he had worn for 20 years. When someone told him of men who had dozens of neckties, he responded, "For just one neck?"

DISTRACTION: This is the most dangerous pitfall, because it is so subtle. Now that you have money to travel on weekends, church gets pushed aside a little. You are required to work longer evenings, so you rationalize that your kids are proud of you and understand why you are not there for prayers at night. You face sleepless nights, unsolvable problems, and jealous people who put pressure on you. You keep saying, "We've got to slow down," but it doesn't get any better. One day you realize your spiritual resources are depleted.

Good News: Prosperity Is for a Purpose

God does not grant certain people a measure of success to reward them for their good behavior. In fact, success is not always an indication of righteousness. God allows it to rain on the just and the unjust, and more often than not it is the unrighteous who find themselves in places of prominence. But God does grant success to righteous people for a reason—that his purpose might be accomplished or his glory revealed. God promises to use your prosperity for his glory if you let him.

When God chooses to give you a certain amount of prosperity or success, recognize that he has done so to reveal his glory or to accomplish his purpose. Watch for him to reveal to you what that purpose might be. Even if you are unable to see it in this life, God has you where you are for a purpose. Look for opportunities to use your success for God's glory.

—Adapted from *Life Preservers,* by Bob Russell

"But God sent me ahead of you to preserve for you a remnant on earth and to save your lives by a great deliverance. So then, it was not you who sent me here, but God. He made me father to Pharaoh, lord of his entire household and ruler of all Egypt" (Genesis 45:7, 8).

Using Prosperity for God's Purposes

Joseph . . .
- was diligent on the job for a prolonged period
- remained faithful to his wife, and grateful for children
- used his position to benefit others
- understood God as the source of his prosperity

WITH GOD'S HELP . . .	Rarely	Sometimes	Usually
I use my prosperity (globally speaking) to benefit others.			
I make a habit of not indulging myself every time I want something.			
I have people in my life who have known me for a long time, who know the "real me."			
I ask God how he wants to use me in my position at work or in the neighborhood.			
I try to be diligent at my current task rather than always looking for more excitement and attention.			
I make an effort to maintain close relationships with the "permanent" people in my life (spouse, children, parents, friends, co-workers).			
I ask God to bring satisfaction into my life's routine so I can remain diligent.			
I regularly give away part of what I make and part of what I have accumulated.			
I look for quiet, subtle ways that Christ can use me every day at work or in the neighborhood.			
I understand that it's important to give back to people who have supported me.			
I understand that it's important to give to people who are younger than me who need the support I wish I had.			

What Joseph Did Right

WHAT JOSEPH DID RIGHT	REFERENCE
Diligent on the job for a prolonged period	
Remained faithful to his wife, grateful for his children (gracious even to brothers who betrayed him)	
Used his position to benefit others	
Understood God as the source of his prosperity	

FILLING IN THE GAPS

TODAY'S PASSAGES	IMPORTANT BACKGROUND
Genesis 41:46–57	Joseph's brothers had sold him into slavery in Egypt because they were jealous of him. Then he was wrongly accused of rape by the wife of an employer who had trusted him implicitly. For several years, he sat in jail before he was called before Pharaoh to interpret a dream, which he did successfully.
Genesis 45:1–11	Joseph's brothers came to Egypt looking for grain and didn't recognize their brother, now a ruler.
Genesis 50:15–23	He moved the entire family to Egypt. Jacob blessed Joseph's sons and Jacob later died.

Eleven

God's Promises in Times of Grief

A friend of mine told me his second Christmas without his wife was more difficult than the first. His wife had died near Thanksgiving, and the first Christmas he had many friends watching out for him, keeping him busy, and encouraging him. The next Christmas he felt more confident he could handle things. He did not plan as many activities to help him deal with his grief, and he was blindsided with memories of past Christmases with his wife.

Life is never the same. There are changes and adjustments, and the loss is always there. But life does resume and become worthwhile again.

—Adapted from *Life Preservers,* by Bob Russell

Central Theme	God helps us move through grief, allowing us to speak to him honestly so we can find fellowship in him.
Lesson Aim	Group members will look at how God helps people through the process of grief and consider ways to approach God honestly with grief.
Bible Background	Job 1:1–22; 2:7–10; 3:1–16; 6:2–4; 42:1–6, 12–15
For Further Study	Read Chapter 11 of *Life Preservers.*

Classes

Building Community

Give a twistie to each class member. (Twisties are the papered wires used to close the ends of plastic bags. If you can easily obtain chenille wires—also called pipe cleaners—use them instead since their length gives students more material to work with.) Instruct class members, **Bend your twistie into a shape that somehow describes how you feel about grief. For example, you could shape it into an arrow because when you lost your job, the grief felt like an arrow going through your heart.** Mention these other occasions for grief: being robbed, losing possessions in a disaster, a friend moving away, losing a position of importance, being forced to retire, changing churches because of a move, loss of health.

Ask class members, **What are some ideas about grief that people have that aren't really true—at least they aren't true to your experience?** Two examples are:
- A wife who has lost a husband doesn't want people to talk to her about him. (She often does.)
- If you're mature, you get over your job loss quickly. (Grieving always takes time.)

You may also wish to mention the occasions for grief listed in the "Wire Sculpture" activity.

Considering Scripture

Display <u>Transparency 11A</u>, "Moving Through Grief," and explain that the lower portion lists the commonly accepted stages of grief. Ask a volunteer to read the background at the top of the transparency, and then explain, **After someone reads each passage listed, we'll stop to consider, In which of these stages of grief did Job appear to be when he spoke in this passage? This may or may not follow the order on this transparency.**

Class members may not agree on the same category. The goal is to examine Job's heart, not make him fit twentieth century grief theory. Begin by having someone read *Job 1:20–22* and offer this example: **Either Job was already into acceptance or he was so shocked that he mouthed a platitude that sounded**

Wire Sculpture
10 Minutes

Option
Grief Myths
10 Minutes

Job's Stages of Grief
10–15 Minutes

> **Materials You'll Need For This Session**
>
> Resource Sheets 11A–11C, Transparency 11A, pens or pencils, chalk and chalkboard, twisties or chenille wires (pipe cleaners)

like acceptance or he was feeling a lot of both. (Write 1:20–22 and the key words, "The Lord gives and the Lord takes away," on the transparency after "shock" and "acceptance." Tearing his robe and shaving his head could have been a sign of "anger," but more likely hurt, which isn't one of these steps.) After each reading, write the reference and a few key words after each of the stages suggested by class members. Here are some thoughts on suggested categories.

2:7–10: Once again, Job was either accepting things well, or he was perhaps in denial—refusing to believe it all happened, unable to face the reality of it. It's as if he shushed his wife, saying, "It's not a problem—really!"

3:1–16: Job cursed the day he was born, and asked, "Why?" five times (vv. 11, 12, 16, 20, 23). He seems to have been in the "anger" stage.

6:2–4: "Depression" is an appropriate category.

42:1–6: "Acceptance" is an appropriate category.

Read the epilogue for the class.

OPTION
Sentence Prayers
10–15 Minutes

Write these passages on the chalkboard: ***Job 1:20–22; 2:7–10; 3:1–16; 6:2–4; 42:1–6***. Then read the introduction from <u>Transparency 11A</u> (you don't have to display it), and explain, **After someone reads each passage, we'll stop to consider, If you could condense Job's attitude or the cry of his heart into a one-sentence prayer, what would it be?** Have someone read Job 1:20–22, and offer this example: From his actions (tearing his robe, shaving his head), his prayer might be, "God, I am devastated," but from his words (v. 21), his prayer might be, "That's OK, God. I'm fine."

Ask the same question about each passage after it is read.

OPTION
Can of Worms Question
10–15 Minutes

Write this question on the chalkboard: **What, if anything, did Job do wrong?** Offer the following ideas, keeping in mind that your goal is not to answer the question, but to provoke thought. Distribute copies of <u>Resource Sheet 11A</u>, "Was Job Wrong?" and have someone read the summary of what happened in the chapters mentioned (right column).

Ask class members what they think. If you wish, ask this question to further stimulate discussion: **Did Job allow his desire to understand why he was suffering overwhelm him and make him question God himself?**

To close the discussion, say, **The book of Job is difficult to understand. One thing is clear, however. Job is a good example of how we can work through grief in an honest way and come out closer to God than ever. It's a stretch to trust God when it looks like he's not taking care of us. Grief stretches our faith and helps us believe that knowing God is always enough in life.**

TAKING THE NEXT STEP

⊞ Distribute copies of Resource Sheet 11B, "How Do I Approach God in My Grief?" Ask class members to take turns reading the handout, and ask them to underline one or two key words as it's being read. Then ask them to tell their words. Accept all answers, but if "honesty" and "nearer to him" in the last paragraph aren't mentioned, point those out.

⊞ Distribute copies of Resource Sheet 11C, "Praying Through Crises," and divide the class into five groups. Assign each group one of the situations on the resource sheet. Explain, **Read your situation and design an honest prayer of grief for the character(s).** Display again Transparency 11A and remind the groups that the stages of grief include anger and depression. Appoint a recorder for each group and ask that person to write the prayer on the back of the resource sheet.

After a few minutes, ask each group to read its prayer.

⊞ Divide the class into groups of four or five each, and ask each group to work on a proverb (a short, pithy saying) that expresses the acceptance phase of grief. That proverb should include the word *God* or a thought regarding God. Offer these examples: "God + nothing = always enough." Or, "Not, 'Why, me, God?' but 'Love me, God!'"

⊞ Before class, talk with three people who have gone through grief for any reason (not just death of a loved one). Ask them to be prepared to tell the class about how their grieving process affected their relationship with God or how God worked in the process. Or, they can tell you, and you will report it to the class. At this point in the session, ask them to come up front and talk for two minutes, or give a report of what they said. Then ask class members if they have questions for one or more of the panelists. Thank the panelists for their cooperation.

Key Word Search
5 Minutes

Honest Prayers
10–15 Minutes

OPTION
Proverbs of Acceptance
10–15 Minutes

OPTION
Panel
10–15 Minutes

PLAN TWO

Groups

BUILDING COMMUNITY

1. What taste (bitter, tart, bland, salty, and so on) do you associate with the idea of grief? (Give this example: grief over death may seem like milk of magnesia—chalky, bland, void of flavor.)

2. OPTION: **What does it mean to "handle grief well"? People tend to think that if someone doesn't appear to be bothered by a circumstance (being robbed, losing possessions in a disaster, a friend moving away, losing a position of importance, being forced to retire, changing churches because of a move, loss of health), they've "handled it well." How true is that?**

CONSIDERING SCRIPTURE

Read Job 1:1–19, or read aloud the summary of this passage from the top of <u>Transparency 11A</u>.

Read Job 1:20–22; 2:7–10.

1. What signs of grief did Job show when he heard the terrible news?

2. What signs of "handling it well" did he give?

3. Was it true, as Job implied in 2:10, that this "trouble" came from God? (No and yes. It came directly from Satan, but God did allow it.)

Read Job 3:1–16.

4. What might Job have been feeling to have cursed the day of his birth?

5. How do Job's three "Why?" questions compare with the "Why?" questions most people ask when grieving over a situation? (Most people want to know why the tragedy happened, but Job wondered why he was born. Job's friends assumed they knew why the tragedy happened—because Job sinned. Job then asked God why he didn't pardon him, 7:21.)

> **Materials You'll Need For This Session**
>
> Resource Sheet 11B, Transparency 11A (optional)

OPTION
Accountability Partners

Have accountability partners meet during the week to discuss their personal experiences with grief. They can discuss these questions: Have those experiences drawn them closer to God? Have they created any bitterness with God? Ask them to pray for each other in their acceptance of what God has done.

OPTION
Worship Ideas

Read Psalm 31 together as an act of worship.

OPTION
Memory Verse

"My eyes had heard of you, but now my eyes have seen you" (Job 42:5).

Read Job 6:2–4.

6. What feelings or attitudes does Job seem to be experiencing?

Read Job 42:1–6.

7. What good things did Job say about God?

8. What did Job say he did that he wished he hadn't?

9. Why do you think Job was ready to repent?

Read Job 42:12–15.

10. Even though Job was blessed more at the end than at the beginning, how would you guess his life was different? (Be sure to include the idea that Job bonded with God in a special way during the grief, based on 42:5: "My ears had heard of you but now my eyes have seen you.")

TAKING THE NEXT STEP

Distribute copies of <u>Resource Sheet 11B</u>, "How Do I Approach God in My Grief?" Then give each group member an index card.

1. Write a prayer for an imaginary person who is going through grief for some reason. (Reiterate reasons for grief from Question 2 of "Building Community"). **Don't be afraid to write prayers that might seem too difficult to pray or even somehow inappropriate.**

After a few minutes, collect the cards and mix them up. Then pass them out and ask group members to read the card they received. Give each group member another index card.

2. Write a prayer of grief for a past or present sadness based on what we've seen in Job's honesty and close relationship with God.

Was Job Wrong?

JOB WAS TESTED
Job 1–2

Job lost everything—oxen, donkeys, sheep, camels, and servants. Even his grown children died.

THREE FRIENDS COUNSELED JOB
Job 3–31

Three friends tried to help Job, but they said these tragedies happened because he had sinned. Scripture says that wasn't so, but they thought it was. So they tried to get him to repent. He refused.

A YOUNG MAN COUNSELED JOB
Job 32–37

Elihu had listened to the conversation and said that the friends were wrong, but Job had become proud and the suffering humbled him. Job still wasn't satisfied that he had found the answer.

GOD ANSWERED JOB
Job 38–41

God answered Job, asking him questions that indicated that God alone is wise enough or powerful enough to create the world and make decisions. He made it clear Job needed to trust him.

JOB WAS RESTORED
Job 42

Job acknowledged that God is supreme and opened himself to a deeper relationship with God.

How Do I Approach God In My Grief?

JOB ASKED, "Lord, why did you even let me be born if you knew I was going to have to experience all this pain?" God could have angrily rejected Job for having the nerve to question him. But God not only came to Job and answered his prayers, he returned to Job all his wealth—twice as much as he had before the tragedy—and gave him ten additional children.

C. S. Lewis, a brilliant apologist for the Christian faith, was a bachelor until the middle of his life. Then he found near ecstatic happiness and a feeling of completion in his brief marriage to a woman who died of cancer a few years later. He wrote a book, *A Grief Observed,* and published it under a pseudonym. Perhaps he feared that it would seem out of character for a man with strong faith, who had helped others through their doubts about God, to write so honestly about his grief.

Lewis wrote, "Oh God, God, why did you take such trouble to force this creature out of its shell if it is now doomed to crawl back—to be sucked back into it?" Lewis said one strange consequence of his loss was that he constantly realized that he was causing embarrassment to the people he'd meet. Wherever he went, he'd notice people walking toward him and could see by their expressions that they were trying to decide if they should say something or not. "I hate it if they do and if they don't," he said.

A widow might get angry at her dead husband when her car breaks down for leaving her with such a mess. A loved one who is grieving is tempted to get angry at the doctors for not doing more or at the person who was driving who caused the accident. A person might feel bitterness toward God for not preventing the tragedy.

The kind of honesty that Job expressed does not drive us from God; it brings us nearer to him. We have a Spirit that intercedes for us with groans and utterances we cannot understand. God loves us and hurts when we hurt. He has promised to comfort us, though the comforting process may take a while.

—Adapted from *Life Preservers,* by Bob Russell

Praying Through Crises

Gary and Susan were the victims of a ferocious tornado. Susan ran to an inner wall and found safety. Gary was outside and held on to the tire of his car. As the car lifted from the ground, a tree fell and pinned the car down. After the tornado was over, Susan and Gary found each other in the front yard and embraced. They are grieving the loss of all their possessions.

Ron and his sister have parted ways after their parents' death. She is upset with what she perceives as injustice in the way their parents designated their possessions in the will. She says Ron is responsible for the unfairness. Ron sees another side of it, but he has tried to make peace. His sister told him she never wants to see him again and has left town. Ron is grieving the loss of a relationship with his sister.

Candace was hired to head a new division in an electronics firm. The firm moved her across the country. She fought hard for respect and got her staff working harmoniously when a merger occurred and she was forced out. She is grieving the loss of her income and challenging position.

Dan and Cindy helped start a church ten years ago. As the church grew, so did they. Both were leaders, teaching the Bible and helping people. Now, they've been relocated across town by their company. They tried commuting, but it's not the same. They keep visiting churches in their new suburb, but they feel lost. They are grieving the loss of their church family.

Nadine's joint disease has gotten worse as she's gotten older. Now she realizes that it is too painful to drive. She feels she can manage the pain itself, but everything else is too much. She can't go anywhere without making elaborate transportation plans. She misses her former leisure activities and rarely sees her friends. She mourns the loss of her freedom, recreation, and close friends.

Moving Through GRIEF

BACKGROUND:

Job was a very rich man. With all that he owned, his financial worth would amount to about six million dollars today. He was also righteous and feared God. All at once through thieves and natural disasters, he lost all of his oxen, donkeys, sheep, camels, and servants. All ten of his grown children died (Job 1:1–19).

Job's Responses:

| 1:20–22 | 2:7–10 | 3:1–16 | 6:2–4 | 42:1–6 |

Epilogue:

God gave Job even more sheep, camels, oxen, donkeys, and ten more children (Job 42:12–15)

In which of these stages of grief did Job appear to be in the above passages?

SHOCK

DENIAL (also bargaining with God)

ANGER

DEPRESSION

ACCEPTANCE

Twelve

God's Promises When Facing Death

*I*n 1993, PGA golf professional Paul Azinger had just won the PGA Championship when he discovered he had cancer. His entire perspective on life radically changed. He said that as he was lying on an X-ray table he was hit by a terrible fear: he could die from cancer. But then, he said, something else even more important occurred to him. He wrote, "I'm going to die eventually anyway. Whether from cancer or something else, I'm definitely going to die. It's just a question of when."

Azinger said that everything he had ever accomplished in golf suddenly became meaningless to him. More than anything else, he wanted to live. Then he remembered something Larry Moody, who leads the Bible study on the pro tour, once said: "Zinger, we're not in the land of the living going to the land of the dying. We're in the land of the dying, going to the land of the living."

—Adapted from *Life Preservers,* by Bob Russell

Central Theme	God promises that death will be a time of comfort and blessings, which means that Christians can face it with confidence.
Lesson Aim	Group members will examine apprehensions about death, discover that confidence before death is possible, and examine the promises made about death.
Bible Background	2 Timothy 4:6–8
For Further Study	Read Chapter 12 of *Life Preservers.*

Classes

Materials You'll Need For This Session

Resource Sheets 12A and 12B, Transparency 12A, pens or pencils, chalk and chalkboard

BUILDING COMMUNITY

Read the introduction to this lesson (p. 133) aloud and then repeat the last sentence, beginning with, "We're not in the land of the living . . ." Ask class members, **What do you think Moody meant by this earth being "the land of the dying"?** If you wish, ask these questions also, **Why is this life the "land of the dying"? Why do we have such trouble recognizing the afterlife as the "land of the living"?**

Quote Reaction
5–7 Minutes

Ask the class to recall jokes that start out with someone appearing (usually with St. Peter) at the pearly gates. Try to collect a few before class to get people going. Conclude by saying, **A lot of our joking about the "pearly gates" is for fun, but it also shows how much we don't know about what will happen after death. Today's session addresses that issue.**

OPTION
Pearly Gates Jokes
5–7 Minutes

Ask class members to help you list at least five ways of talking about death in pleasant terms. For example, when someone says, "our *departed* loved one," they don't mean someone who has gone away, but someone who is deceased or dead. Close by asking, **Why are euphemisms used in talking about death?** (For many, death is unpleasant and so it is masked. Others fear the unknown and so euphemisms help. Still others may have confidence about death—especially if they're older— and so the pleasant language is appropriate.)

OPTION
Listing Euphemisms
5 Minutes

CONSIDERING SCRIPTURE

Ask the class to turn to *2 Timothy 4:6–8,* and have someone read it aloud. Ask class members to suggest one word that sums up Paul's attitude toward death based on this passage. Here are some possibilities:
- *prepared, confident*—Paul described how in his life he had "fought," "finished," and "kept." He was confident that "now there is in store for me . . ."
- *positive*—Paul viewed death as "my departure" and expected a "crown of righteousness."
- *expectant, eager*—Paul expected a "crown of righteousness" and spoke of those who "longed for [Christ's] appearing."

One Word Summaries
5 Minutes

Display <u>Transparency 12A</u>, "It's Not Dying I'm Afraid of, But . . ." and explain, **The common attitude toward death is very different from Paul's attitude. Listed here are some common fears. Are there others that should be listed?** Write their responses on the transparency in the space provided at the bottom.

Distribute copies of <u>Resource Sheet 12A</u>, "God's Promises About Facing Death." Ask class members to draw from the Scriptures printed there to offer ideas about how to answer these apprehensions. Write their suggestions on Transparency 12A, if you wish.

Here are some suggestions from Resource Sheet 12A:

Fear listed on Transparency 12A	Assurance from Resource Sheet 12A
The painful events that could lead up to death	Scripture and thoughts under heading, *You will receive comfort in the valley of death.*
Not knowing where I'll be	See, *You will immediately be in the presence of the Lord.*
Not knowing what will happen to my body and spirit	See, *Your spirit will depart from your body* and *You will be given a new, perfect body.*
Not knowing what Heaven will really be like	See, *You will inherit a heavenly home.*

Have class members turn to *2 Timothy 4:6–8,* and ask someone to read it aloud. Then distribute paper and pencils or pens and ask class members to paraphrase these verses in their own words. You may want to ask them to paraphrase it in a style that would be meaningful to a certain segment of the population: wording it for small children or for gang members or for corporate executives, for instance. Ask class members to read their paraphrases.

TAKING THE NEXT STEP

Be sensitive in this portion especially to those who aren't Christians. They may have very different thoughts about this—even more questions, skepticism, fear, or self-condemnation.

Ask class members, **Which colors do you associate with being confident, positive, expectant? Why?** Then pick two of the colors most frequently chosen (for example, blue and yellow) and write sentences such as these on the chalkboard:

- Blue is a good color for death because . . .
- Yellow is a good color for death because . . .

Then say, **Death is often associated with the color black because people wear black clothes for mourning. Let's adjust that a little. Complete these sentences based on facts or ideas we've learned today. Feel free to get ideas from Resource Sheet 12A, "God's Promises About Facing Death." Qualify this, if necessary, as describing the death of Christians who go to be with God.**

Ask class members to go over the truths on <u>Resource Sheet 12A</u>, "God's Promises About Facing Death," and underline the phrases that give them a positive, confident, expectant sense toward death. Then ask them to pull out one or two of those phrases to meditate on there in the classroom. Allow two or three minutes of silence for this.

OPTION
Meditation
5 Minutes

Distribute copies of <u>Resource Sheet 12B</u>, "Letter from God." Explain, **Fill in your own name at the top. Complete the first sentence by writing about your apprehensions about death. Then complete the next sentence with words of comfort and confidence you may have found in today's session. Feel free to get ideas from Resource Sheet 12A, "God's Promises About Facing Death."** After they've finished, ask a few to volunteer to read their letters.

OPTION
Letter from God
5 Minutes

Groups

BUILDING COMMUNITY

1. How has the media made death seem more scary? (Be open to a wide range of responses—books and movies about vampires, newspaper accounts of deaths in natural disasters, books and movies that portray the afterlife, blood and guts movies.)

2. What, if any, book or movie have you experienced that gave you a positive feeling about death or the afterlife?

3. What would it take for us to feel more confident about being with God in the afterlife?

CONSIDERING SCRIPTURE

Read 2 Timothy 4:6–8.

1. How did Paul view his life at that point?

2. What did Paul look forward to?

3. How did Paul seem to feel about his eventual death?

Present photocopies of Resource Sheet 12A, "God's Promises About Facing Death," and ask a group member to read it.

4. What appears to happen to the spirit once the body dies? (See the second and third points, especially 2 Corinthians 5:8; Luke 23:46; Acts 7:59; and Luke 16:22.)

5. Describe what the new body will be like. (See the fourth point, especially 1 Corinthians 15:42, 44, 51, 52.)

6. Describe from Scripture what Heaven will be like. (See the fifth point, especially John 14:2, 3 and Revelation 21:4.)

7. What does God tell us that helps us with fears of what might happen leading up to death? (Besides all the above, we will receive comfort. See the first point.)

Materials You'll Need For This Session

A bow used in wrapping gifts or a gift-wrapped box, Resource Sheet 12A

OPTION
Accountability Partners
Have partners meet and discuss all three questions under "Taking the Next Step." Ask them to include in their discussions any encouragement they received from today's session.

OPTION
Worship Ideas
Read Psalm 23 together as an act of worship.

OPTION
Memory Verse
"Now there is in store for me the crown of righteousness, which the Lord, the righteous Judge, will award to me on that day—and not only to me, but also to all who have longed for his appearing" (2 Timothy 4:8).

TAKING THE NEXT STEP

Bring a gift bow, or, if you have time, a gift-wrapped box.

1. What gift of confidence has God given you today about life after death or going through death? (Ask group members to hold the gift or bow as they talk and pass it on to the next person who wants to speak.)

2. Who in your life has died to whom it would be helpful to apply these truths? (For example, if a class member knows people who were in pain as they died, it might help to know that God provided comfort.)

3. What prayers can we offer when we ponder death and feel apprehensive?

God's Promises About Facing Death

✦ *You will receive comfort in the valley of death.*

God is with us through whatever difficult circumstances might precede our death. "Even though I walk through the valley of the shadow of death, I will fear no evil, for you are with me; your rod and your staff, they comfort me" (Psalm 23:4).

✦ *Your spirit will depart from your body.*

Paul referred to death as being **"away from the body"** (2 Corinthians 5:8). Paul called his death a **"departure,"** using a nautical term that pictured a ship sailing out to sea (2 Timothy 4:6). Your body is just an outer casing for the real you—your spirit. Just as a hand animates a glove, it is the spirit that energizes a body. When the spirit departs, the body, like a lifeless glove, is thrown aside.

✦ *You will immediately be in the presence of the Lord.*

Paul said to be away from the body was to be **"at home with the Lord"** (2 Corinthians 5:8). When Jesus died, he prayed, **"Father, into your hands I commit my spirit"** (Luke 23:46). When Stephen was stoned to death, he looked toward Heaven and said, **"Lord Jesus, receive my spirit"** (Acts 7:59). In Jesus' parable, a beggar named Lazarus died and was immediately comforted at **"Abraham's side"** (Luke 16:22). When a preacher I knew died, he said just before he departed, "I see it! Do you see it? It's beautiful!"

✦ *You will be given a new, perfect body.*

When Jesus died on the cross, his body was placed in a tomb, but his spirit was not there. His spirit returned to the body three days later when it was brought back to life. The body he had after his resurrection was not the same body he had before the resurrection. Jesus ate food after his resurrection and could be seen and touched, but Jesus did some things after his resurrection he had not previously done: He appeared and disappeared suddenly; he entered a room without opening the door; he ascended into Heaven before them. **"The body that is sown is perishable, it is raised imperishable; . . . it is sown a natural body, it is raised a spiritual body. . . . We will not all sleep, but we will all be changed—in a flash, in the twinkling of an eye, at the last trumpet. For the trumpet will sound, the dead will be raised imperishable, and we will be changed"** (1 Corinthians 15:42, 44, 51, 52).

✦ *You will inherit a heavenly home.*

"In my Father's house are many rooms; if it were not so, I would have told you. I am going there to prepare a place for you. And if I go and prepare a place for you, I will come back and take you to be with me that you also may be where I am" (John 14:2, 3). Heaven is described as a place where there is no crying, no pain, no sorrow, no death (Revelation 21:4).

—Adapted from *Life Preservers,* by Bob Russell

Letter from God

Dear _____,
(your name)

I know that what scares you most about death is . . .

Don't be scared. Try to be confident because . . .

It's Not *Dying* I'm Afraid of, But . . .

- The painful events that could lead up to it

    - Not knowing what will happen next, such as . . .

- Not knowing where I'll be

    - Not knowing what will happen to my body and spirit

- Not knowing what Heaven will really be like

Thirteen

God's Promises in Times of Waiting

I promise." In a hedonistic world where people would rather do what they feel like doing than keep their word, that phrase may seem pretty meaningless—unless the promise comes from a loving father.

We have a perfect heavenly Father. Is there anyone on earth as loving and unselfish as God? Does anyone care more about you than he does? Is there anyone who is more true to his word? Is there anyone who has sacrificed more for you? When God makes a promise, you can believe he will do what he says—no matter what.

—Adapted from *Life Preservers*, by Bob Russell

Central Theme	Because God keeps his promises, times of waiting aren't filled with sluggish inactivity, but with alertness, expectancy, and a willingness to do whatever is required.
Lesson Aim	Group members will examine biblical principles about God as a promise keeper and consider how they can wait expectantly for God to fulfill his promises.
Bible Background	Matthew 24:42—25:13; 2 Peter 3:9
For Further Study	Reread the introduction of *Life Preservers* and review chapters as necessary.

Classes

BUILDING COMMUNITY

Distribute photocopies of <u>Resource Sheet 13A</u>, "Keeping a Promise—No Matter What," and say to class members, **How would this story come across as a movie? What would the lines sound like? For example, what would the dialogue sound like at these moments:**

1. What the father said when he saw the building flattened
2. What the wife (who had probably come there by this time) said when the police officer and firefighter told the father to go home
3. What the father said to people who tried to convince him to go home after he'd been digging for twenty-four hours
4. What the other kids said to Armand when his father dug them out

If you have twenty or more people in your class, divide the class into groups of ten. Have the class or groups sit in a circle. Ask for a volunteer, explaining that the volunteer will have the easiest job. After someone has volunteered in each circle, ask him or her to say something about waiting. Explain, **The next person in the circle (clockwise) must pick up on what the first one said. Start with the words, "That reminds me of . . ."** **Finish that sentence with a famous saying about waiting or a story about waiting or an example of someone who could or couldn't wait.** (Anything related to waiting will do.) The point is to get class members to start thinking about the topic of waiting and how frustrating it can be.

CONSIDERING SCRIPTURE

Ask someone to read *Matthew 24:42—25:13* aloud, and then have the class divide into groups of five. Give each group paper and a pen or pencil. Ask the groups to write a job description of the "faithful and wise servant," describing especially how this servant behaves while waiting.

Here are some items they might suggest: keeping watch (24:42, 43); doing assigned tasks (feeding the other servants, 24:45–47); not shirking or neglecting duties (24:48–51); being prepared (25:1–13); thinking ahead (25:1–13).

Responding to a Story
5–7 Minutes

Materials You'll Need For This Session

Resource Sheets 13A–13C, Transparency 13A, pens or pencils, chalk and chalkboard

Circular Conversation
10 Minutes

Job Description
15 Minutes

Ask someone to read *2 Peter 3:9*. Say, **This verse promises that God keeps his promises promptly—or as promptly as he deems necessary. How do we cultivate a deeper belief that God keeps his promises?** (Class members may suggest studying Bible passages about this, praying about it, hearing stories of others to whom God has kept his promises.)

Display Transparency 13A, "Believing that God Keeps His Promises," and read the three parts of the circle and the summary statements at the bottom. Give class members a few minutes to absorb this truth. Summarize it in these words, if you wish: **The more we want to depend on God, the better we can wait with alertness and willingness to do what is required. The more we "actively wait," the more we depend on God.**

TAKING THE NEXT STEP

Distribute copies of Resource Sheet 13B, "God's Promises in Troubled Times," and explain that this is a list of promises God has made to us. (It corresponds to the lessons in this series and the chapters in *Life Preservers*.)

Explain, **With each of these promises, it becomes overwhelming to sort out what it means to do our part, but depend on God to resolve the situation. Here's a work sheet to help you consider this.** Distribute copies of Resource Sheet 13C, "Active Waiting."

Direct class members' attention to the first row below the headings on 13C. Let's say that my problem is not only that my son is on drugs, but that I live in fear that he will die or be a drug addict for the rest of his life. It's important to sort out "my part" (how to wait expectantly, doing what is within my power to do) from "God's part" (things over which I have no control). Have someone read "My Part," and then "God's Part." Ask if there's anything else that needs to be added to either column.

Then ask class members to suggest another specific problem and relate it to one of God's promises. (They may wish to refer to Resource Sheet 13B for ideas.) Have them write it at the bottom of the first column. Discuss what is "my part" (active waiting) and what is God's part. Urge them to write down their ideas. Work through several problems if you have time. For help with "God's part," find the category on Resource Sheet 13B, left column, into which the problem falls. Check the right column for the promise God makes concerning this issue.

Finally, ask class members to choose a problem from their own lives and work through the process on Resource Sheet 13C, sorting out what is "my part" and "God's part." Give them a few minutes to work. Summarize, **Whatever you have written under "My**

Part" is what God has put in your "in basket," so to speak. This is your task in the days ahead. The work under God's part is for him to do and for you to depend on him to do.

Ask class members to sit quietly for a minute or two, pondering the promises on Resource Sheet 13B, "God's Promises in Troubled Times." Ask them then to circle the promise on the page that God seems to be telling them they need to cling to most. Say, **While you're being quiet, imagine for a minute what you would look like if you were holding on to that promise with everything you've got. How would you behave? What kinds of things would you say?** Give them a minute or two more of quiet time to think.

OPTION
Picturing a Promise
5–7 Minutes

Groups

BUILDING COMMUNITY

1. Waiting is normally considered to be a negative, boring thing to do. When, if ever, has waiting been a positive thing for you? (Listen carefully to see if it involved a security that someone was coming for them—similar to the security we learn to feel in God's love.)

OPTION: Distribute photocopies of <u>Resource Sheet 13A</u>, "Keeping a Promise—No Matter What."

2. What do you think the father was thinking at each of the points numbered on the sheet (1–4)?

3. Have you ever attributed those same thoughts to God concerning you?

CONSIDERING SCRIPTURE

Read Matthew 24:42–51.

1. What command is repeated twice in the first two verses?

2. What, in particular, did Jesus want his listeners to keep watch for?

3. In what way does the wicked servant deserve a place with the hypocrites? (He accepted the role as caretaker, but did the opposite.)

Read Matthew 25:1–13.

4. Why do you think Jesus described the five virgins with extra oil as "wise" instead of simply as "prepared"? (They may have somehow guessed that the wait would be long and a lot of oil required, while the others did not.)

5. Based on what you have read, what do you think it means to "keep watch"?

Materials You'll Need For This Session

Resource Sheets 13A and 13B (optional), Transparency 13A

Accountability Partners

Have accountability partners meet and talk about the past few weeks and the promises they've discussed (using Resource Sheet 13B, "God's Promises in Troubled Times," if they have it). Urge them to talk about their growth and what they've seen God do in their lives.

OPTION

Worship Ideas

Read Psalm 130 together as an act of worship.

OPTION

Memory Verse

"The Lord is not slow in keeping his promise, as some understand slowness. He is patient with you, not wanting anyone to perish, but everyone to come to repentance" (2 Peter 3:9).

6. How does this contradict the notion that waiting is something that is inactive?

Read 2 Peter 3:9.

7. What character qualities about God does this passage reveal? (Have someone record their answers, or write them on a chalkboard or large piece of paper. They might suggest:
- dependability—not wishy-washy in keeping promises
- punctuality—knowing the perfectly right time
- patience
- generosity—eager to provide salvation for everyone

TAKING THE NEXT STEP

Distribute copies of Transparency 13A. Look at it together and notice the last sentence on the sheet.

1. How does a person go about doing whatever is necessary (keeping watch) without becoming impatient and interfering with God's timing?

OPTION: Distribute copies of Resource Sheet 13B, "God's Promises in Troubled Times." (If your group has accountability partners, have them save this handout or give extras to those who normally meet.)

2. As you reflect on the times we've met and discussed God's promises, on which of these promises do you think you need to focus most in your life?

Keeping a Promise– No Matter What

In the confusion that followed the 1989 earthquake that flattened Armenia, a father left his wife securely at home and rushed to his son's school. When he arrived, he discovered that the building was flattened. (1)

While looking at what was left, he remembered the promise he had made to his son: "No matter what, I'll always be there for you!" It looked like a hopeless situation, but he could not take his mind off that promise.

He remembered that his son's classroom was in the back right corner of the building. He rushed there and started digging through the rubble. Other grieving parents arrived, crying for their children. Some tried to pull him off the rubble saying, "It's too late! They're dead. You can't help!" Even a police officer and firefighter told him to go home. (2)

Courageously, he proceeded alone because he needed to know for himself whether his boy was dead or alive. He dug for eight hours, then twelve, then twenty-four, (3) then thirty-six hours. Finally, in the thirty-eighth hour, he pulled back a boulder and heard his son's voice. He screamed his son's name, "Armand!"

A voice answered him, "Dad? It's me, Dad!" Then the boy added these priceless words: "I told the other kids not to worry. I told them that if you were alive, you'd save me, and when you saved me, they'd be saved. You promised, 'No matter what, I'll always be there for you.' You did it, Dad!" (4)

God especially wanted you to be comforted during difficult times. He knew that this world is full of heartaches. He knew you would endure your share of earthquakes in this world, and you would need special assurance from him in times of need.

—Adapted from the introduction of *Life Preservers*, by Bob Russell

"The Lord is not slow in keeping his promise, as some understand slowness. He is patient with you, not wanting anyone to perish, but everyone to come to repentance" (2 Peter 3:9).

God's Promises in Troubled Times

Fear
God helps us overcome fear through the testimony of others, the support of godly leaders, and unexplainable circumstances.

Doubt
God works patiently with us to help us overcome doubt.

Loneliness
God responds to our times of loneliness and meets our needs as we learn to trust him, get involved in life, and be patient.

Finances
God promises to provide basic necessities to those who are faithful.

Temptation
If we stay focused on God, we can avoid flirting with temptation, which brings shame and disaster.

Rebellion
God promises discipline for those who rebel and restoration for those who repent.

Guilt
Having a clear conscience helps us admit guilt and confess sin, and knowing Christ helps us find forgiveness.

Worry
God, our compassionate friend, provides provisions one day at a time and the possibility of an incomprehensible peace.

Opposition
Christians can get beyond opposition and criticism by keeping their focus on pleasing Christ instead of pleasing others.

Prosperity
God offers us prosperity in order to do his will in the world and bless others.

Grief
God helps us move through grief, allowing us to speak to him honestly so we can find fellowship in him.

Death
God promises that death will be a time of comfort and blessings so that Christians can face it with confidence.

—Adapted from *Life Preservers*, by Bob Russell

Active Waiting

PROMISE I'D LIKE TO SEE FULFILLED	MY PART (active waiting)	GOD'S PART
• Overcoming fear of son's ruin from drugs	• Pray for son, and ask others to pray for him	• Use unexplainable circumstances to help son become desperate enough to change and want help
	• Seek support from others in my situation	• Help son sense my love and acceptance
	• Accept and love my son no matter what	

Believing That God Keeps His Promises

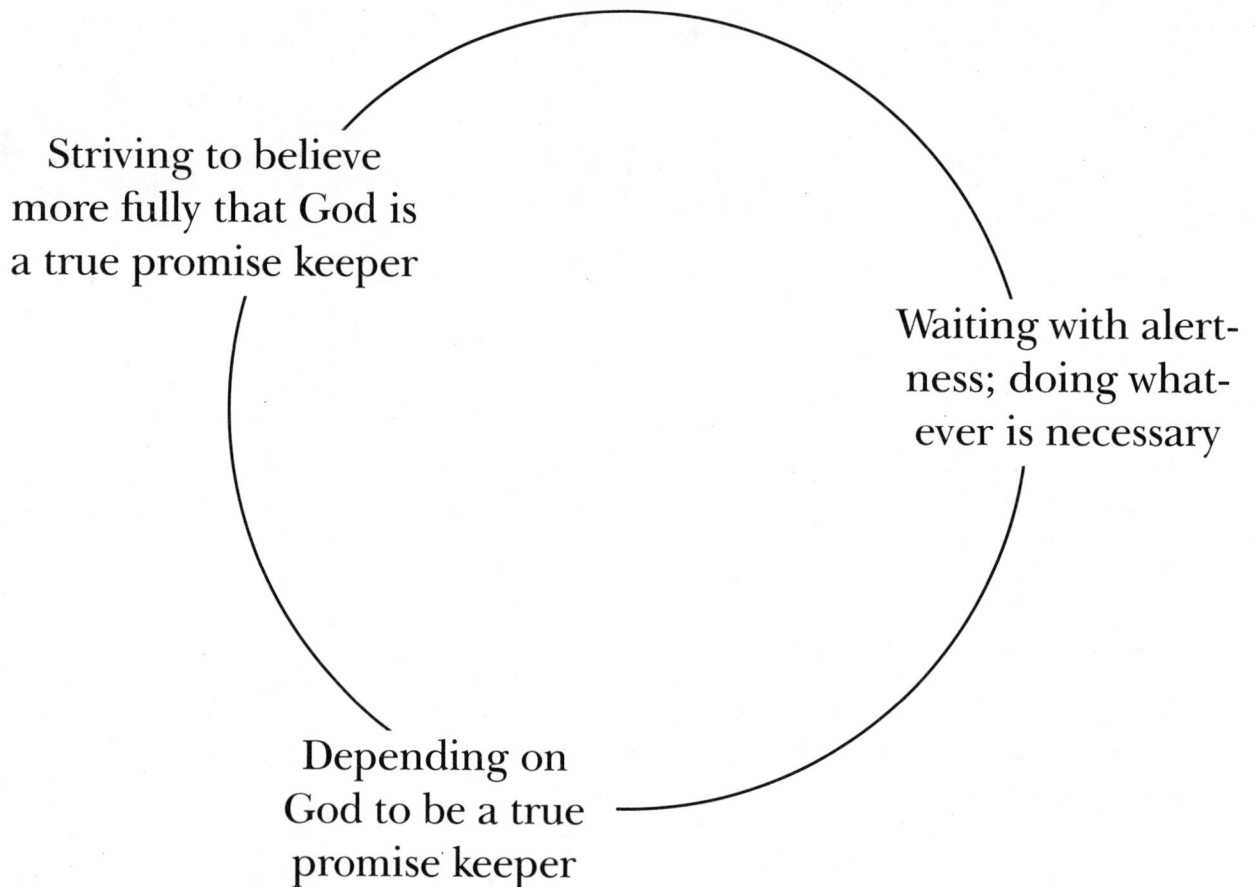

Striving to believe
more fully that God is
a true promise keeper

Waiting with alert-
ness; doing what-
ever is necessary

Depending on
God to be a true
promise keeper

- The more we *believe* in God as an active keeper of his promises, the more likely we are to wait with alertness, *doing* whatever is necessary.

- The more we *do* what is necessary, the more we come to *depend* on God to keep his promises.

Tips for Preparing for a Study

By Michael C. Mack

"There is always a tendency of the body to sabotage the attention of the mind by providing some distraction," the poet Stephen Spender wrote. Who understands that better than a person in a small group or Sunday school meeting who can not focus on spiritual matters because of an uncomfortable atmosphere?

Here are several tips to remember when preparing the physical environment of your meeting to keep participants involved.

• **Meet in a circle,** where everyone is on the same eye-level and can see the face of every other person in the group. A circle helps everyone participate equally.

• **Check the thermostat.** It doesn't take many people in a room to increase the temperature. One expert advises that 67 degrees is an ideal temperature for groups.

• **Sniff around.** We can get so accustomed to the smells in our homes that we don't notice them anymore. Pets, things children spill in odd places, heavy perfumes, last night's dinner, even room deodorizers can irritate people's noses. Also, try lighting a few candles or simmering potpourri in the house. Research has shown, for instance, that peppermint helps keep people alert.

• **Make your meeting tasteful.** Straight-from-the-oven brownies, popcorn, or a beautifully arranged tray of fruit encourage group interaction. They also let people know you want them there and planned ahead. Be creative and remember to provide for weight watchers, diabetics, and others with medical or personal needs.

• **Find the right room size.** A small group meeting may feel intimidating in a huge room. A group of twelve may feel claustrophobic in a very small room.

• **Get close.** Even if you can't sit "knee-to-knee," get as close as everyone feels comfortable.

• **Let your light shine,** but not too brightly. Low lamp lights are better than bright florescent lighting. If you meet in a classroom, try bringing a couple table lamps and use them rather than the overhead lights. It should be bright enough that everyone can read their Bibles, but low enough to feel cozy.

• **Provide Bibles of the same version.** Participants can use their own Bibles, but suggest that everyone use the same version so that everyone can be on the "same page."

• **Be sure each person has his or her own copy of Scripture.**

• **Don't allow couples to share.** One of them will be less involved in the discussion.

• **Guard against distractions.** Turn telephone ringers off (unless parents have small children at baby-sitters and need to be contacted in case of emergency). If children are being watched in the same house as the meeting, be sure they are as much out of hearing range as possible. (Be sure to hire excellent child care providers whom parents can trust.) Put pets in another room or outside. Turn off TV sets, radios, and computers during a meeting.

This article is taken from The Small Group Network Online (http://smallgroups.com). More tips, ideas, and resources for leading a group are available at this World Wide Web site. This ministry is operated by Michael C. Mack, series editor of Standard Publishing's Creative Groups Guides.

Other Creative Groups Guides
from Standard Publishing

PRAISE UNDER PRESSURE
13 complete lessons
Guide by David Faust and Troy Jackson
Study the life of King David to learn how to cope with life's pressures.
Order number 11-40320 *(ISBN 0-7847-0490-2)*

THE NEW TESTAMENT CHURCH THEN AND NOW
13 complete lessons
Guide by Timothy Heck
Learn how today's church can continue the same mission as the first-century church.
Order number 11-40322 *(ISBN 0-7847-0492-9)*

CARRY ON!
13 complete lessons
Guide by Timothy Heck
Find help and hope for life's everyday battles.
Order number 11-40316 *(ISBN 0-7847-0486-4)*

VICTORY IN JESUS
13 complete lessons
Guide by Jan Johnson
Learn to live victoriously in your life in Christ.
Order number 11-40314 *(ISBN 0-7847-0424-4)*

FAITH'S FUNDAMENTALS
7 complete lessons
Guide by Kent C. Odor and Mark Ingmire
Equip class and group members with the seven essentials of Christian belief.
Order number 11-40311 *(ISBN 0-7847-0391-4)*

DREAM INTRUDERS
6 complete lessons
Guide by Tim Sutherland
Help group members learn to get through the difficult times and temporary setbacks in life.
Order number 11-40312 *(ISBN 0-7847-0392-2)*

FIND US FAITHFUL
13 complete lessons
Guide by Michael D. McCann
Learn to pass on your faith to the next generation.
Order number 11-40308 *(ISBN 0-7847-0308-6)*

A CALL TO PRAYER
7 complete lessons
Guide by Jan Johnson
Learn to pray more effectively, more sincerely, with more power, and without hindrances.
Order number 11-40309 *(ISBN 0-7847-0309-4)*

CLAIMING YOUR PLACE
7 complete lessons
Guide by Michael C. Mack and Mark A. Taylor
Help your small group or class learn to find where they fit in the life of the church.
Order number 11-40305 *(ISBN 0-7847-0285-3)*

HEARING GOD
6 complete lessons
Guide by Michael C. Mack and Mark A. Taylor
Help your group or class learn how to read God's Word—and really understand it!
Order number 11-40306 *(ISBN 0-7847-0286-1)*

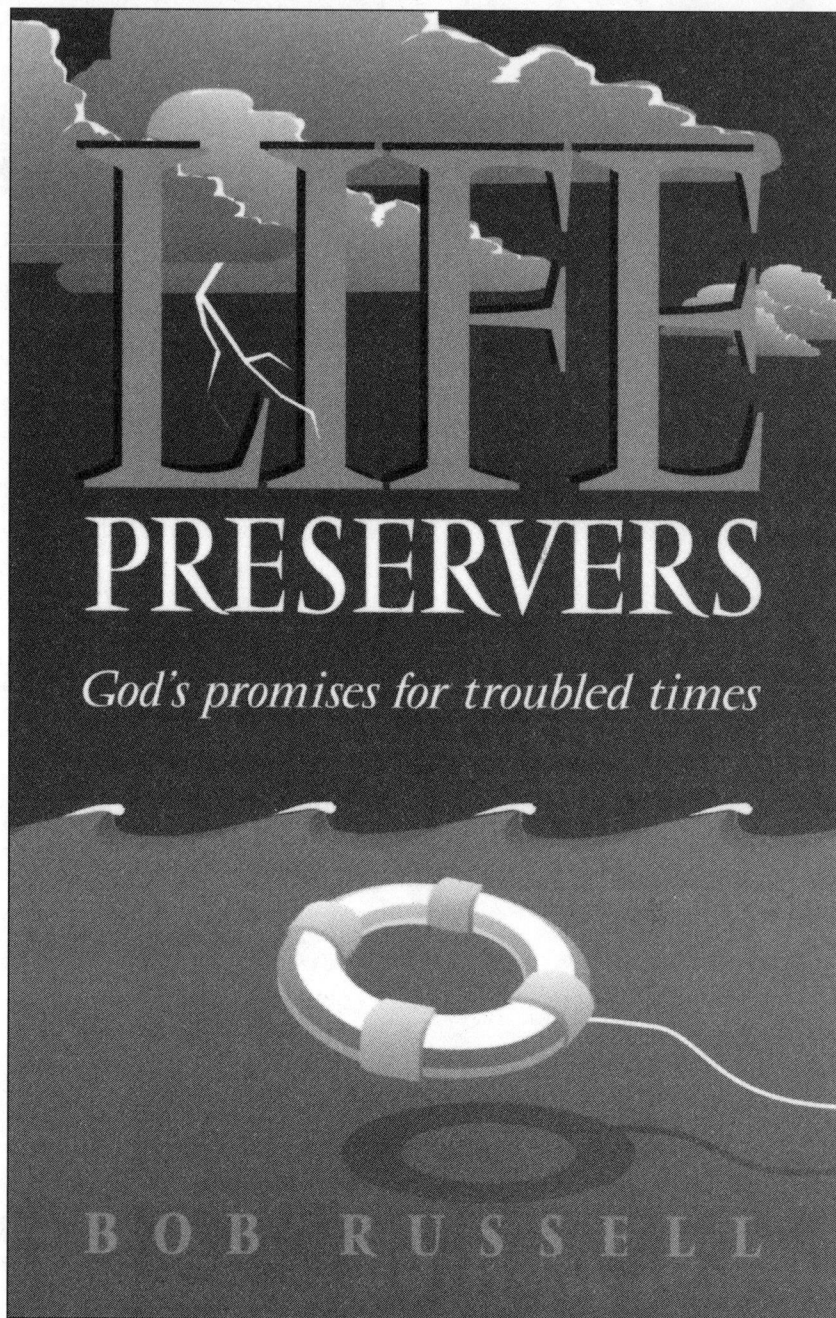